Five Core Principles of the Discipleship Journey

Twenty-One Lessons for Small Groups

Dr. James R. Hicks

Copyright © 2023 by James R. Hicks
ISBN 978-0-9894566-2-3

Published by James Hicks
www.smallgroupinstitute.com
bfcn2@me.com

Printed in the United States of America

Table of Contents

Forward:

It is my privilege to introduce you to this special series of small group studies which support the Journey of Grace and the pursuit of Christlike discipleship. Each study highlights one of the Five Core Principles of discipleship. These Five Core Principles are the result of a series of discussions with Christian discipleship leaders from around the world who were asked, "What principles, practices, habits, lived out, would assure the raising of a generation of Christlike disciples who make Christlike disciples?"

I am very thankful for the passion of Dr. James Hicks, whose years of ministry and expertise in small groups developed this study. His life of servant discipleship and years of diligent study of small groups and scripture have resulted in this work.

Dr. Scott R. Rainey
NDI Global Director

Acknowledgements:

I would like to thank a number of people who were involved in bringing this work to print. I especially want to thank my wife, *Marilyn S. Hicks,* who worked alongside me to bring this work to life. Other contributors include the following: Scott Rainey, Sarah Loganbill, Natasha Skyba, Larry Morris, and Daryll Stanton. Cover designed by Susan M. Sims, author of *Being Transparent with Yourself, God, and Others.*

Introduction:

These small group discipleship lessons focus on the five <u>Core Principles</u> of Nazarene Discipleship International (<u>NDI</u>) in support of its <u>MISSION</u> to carry out the Great Commission to children, youth, and adults in preparation for a lifelong journey of being and making Christlike disciples in the nations. Likewise, its <u>PURPOSE</u> is that of NDI, to assist local churches in:

Reaching non-believers for Jesus,

Establishing new believers in their faith in Christ,

Walking with believers to a fully surrendered, heart-cleansed, fruit-bearing, and Spirit-filled life.

These lessons go hand in hand with the new vision of the Church of the Nazarene for making disciples as a <u>JOURNEY OF GRACE</u>. This path of disciple making, and the church's co-mission with Jesus Christ, is to reach the lost, establish new believers in their faith, and walk with them into the joyous experience with God called entire sanctification. The vision is evangelism with holiness in mind AND holiness with evangelism in mind!

The core of our faith and life is to love God and love others. Everyone committed to the great commission should be **engaged in relationships** that honor God and edify the Body of Christ. Loving relationships help us walk the path of holiness as we receive both encouragement and loving correction.

As we live out these principles in the life and ministries of the local church and in the practices and behaviors of every Nazarene, Christ's followers will accomplish the mission of making Christlike disciples in the nations. Recognizing that discipleship will look different as culture shapes methodologies, the NDI global mission, purpose, and core principles will remain the same. We will look more closely at these in the upcoming sections.

Section 1:

Fervent Prayer

I Love Prayer

As I was thinking about this series of lessons on fervent prayer, I thought about how much I love to pray to my Father each day, and what prayer means to me. I penned the following:

I Love Prayer

Prayer is a relationship to be maintained.
Prayer is a work to be accomplished.
Prayer is a land to be explored.
Prayer is a prize to be won.
Prayer is a hope that forever lives.
Prayer is an experience that is always new.

Prayer is a means to communicate with God.
Prayer is a quiet place where no one else can come.
Prayer is a secure place for the lonely, the needy, the broken, the forgotten,
the one who has been taken advantage of, the one who has been abused,
the one that no one believes in, the one with little purpose,
and the one that has no plan.

Prayer provides a way out of sin and the entangled web that binds.
Prayer provides truth that we could never learn on our own.
Prayer brings life because we are willing to receive it.
Prayer is as natural as taking a breath, as enjoyable as stretching a muscle,
and as soothing as water from a spring.

I continue in prayer because I can speak from my heart and always be understood.
Jesus spoke to His Father in Heaven, and now we, too, give voice
knowing, as the Heavens share in the glory of God, so we absorb what is divine.
Don't linger away from prayer.
It is a fountain for every thirst, a path for all who are willing to find, and a place
where all we ask in His name will be given.

Yes, I love prayer.

by Dr. James R. Hicks
2022

Lesson 1

Fervent Prayer – A Sincere Conversation with God

Scripture: *"For I know the plans I have for you," declares the Lord, "plans to prosper you and not to harm you, plans to give you hope and a future. Then you will call upon me and come and pray to me, and I will listen to you"* (Jeremiah 29:11-12 NIV).

Many people want a quick fix in their time of testing or trouble, and they want their prayers answered quickly. When their prayers are not answered in what they consider a timely manner, they may choose to give up on prayer because the answer did not come immediately. Also, they may give up on prayer because they did not get the answer they wanted.

Prayer is meant to be much more than a cry of desperation. It is having a sincere conversation with our Heavenly Father. That is what it was for Jesus during his time on earth. He did not just pray when he needed a quick answer from his Father. He spoke to his Father, listened for the Father's leading, and was grateful for the Father's presence throughout each day. Jesus had a personal connection to his Father while he was on earth doing his Father's will. He would step away from the crowds and even his disciples to pray. He would get up early to pray to his Father. Praying was not just to get answers – it was to share his life with the ongoing life of God the Father. Jesus protected and never wanted his sacred connection to the Father to be broken or weakened.

I've heard people say they don't really have that much time to pray with everything going on in their lives. My question to them would be: do you make time to eat – do you make time to go to the gym -- do you make time to enroll your kids in sports, etc. – do you make time to spend with your friends -- then you need to make time to spend with your Heavenly Father. He is the giver of life for you, and he is the life you need to share with others. He desires time with you. He wants to talk with you just as you talk to your spouse or your children. He created you so he could have a meaningful relationship with you. That's why he created Adam – to have an ongoing relationship with him. He is our Creator. He desires our time.

Over the next several sessions, we will be studying prayer, more specifically, sincere fervent prayer. Our topics will include fervent prayer: a sincere conversation with God; examples of fervent prayer; personal prayer prints; four attitudes for fervent praying; and when God says no to a prayer. Lastly, we will have a testimonial from this author entitled "I Love Prayer."

In this lesson, we will discover what is prayer, why we use the term fervent prayer, and discuss the benefits from a life of fervent prayer. But first, let's talk about what prayer is.

3

Questions:

When was the first time you remember praying? It could be when you were a child before going to sleep. Maybe it was when you were saved.

Describe how you felt when you were praying. Were you nervous, fearful, guilty, excited, etc.?

Is there a particular verse about prayer that is meaningful to you? If so, what is it and why is it meaningful?

Contemplate:

In Jeremiah 29:12, God speaks to all of us and gives a personal promise. This is called an "if-then" proposition in a court of law: if you call upon me, if you come and pray to me, then I will listen to you.

Jesus' Life of Prayer

Prayer, in simple terms, can be described as talking with God, listening to him, seeking his will, sharing our needs, and thanking him for all he has done for us. It is taking time out of our hectic schedules to focus on our relationship with him.

After Jesus had called his disciples and went throughout Galilee teaching and healing, crowds followed him. When he *"saw the crowds, he went up on a mountainside and sat down. His disciples came to him, and he began to teach them"* (Matthew 5:1-2 NIV). In his Sermon on the Mount, Jesus told his disciples how they should pray in Matthew 6:9-13 KJV. He said, *"After this manner therefore pray ye:*

Our Father which art in heaven,
Hallowed be thy name.
Thy kingdom come,
Thy will be done
in earth, as it is in heaven.
Give us this day our daily bread.
And forgive us our debts,
as we forgive our debtors.

And lead us not into temptation,
but deliver us from evil:
For thine is the kingdom,
and the power, and the glory, forever.
Amen."

Let's Pause:

Since we are studying about prayer, let's take time right now (as a group) to pray the Lord's Prayer together.

Do you notice Jesus did not begin by asking his Father for anything? He began this prayer ascribing to God the praise and honor that only God deserves. How many times do we go to prayer distracted, and it seems we are on a rigid or short time schedule? God deserves our best, not our leftover time.

Question:

What are some attributes or characteristics we could ascribe to our Heavenly Father? It could be *Everlasting Father, Almighty God, Creator, Defender, Protector, Alpha, Omega, Tower of Refuge...the list can go on and on.*

Exercise:

As a group, compile a list with more of God's attributes (characteristics) that can be used during your personal prayer time. Keep this list with you as you pray to God this next week.

Remember, honoring him should come before any of our requests and petitions. When we focus on God, we may find our requests are not as important as we thought they were. Focusing on him reminds us of how great he is, how powerful he is to overcome anything, and how protected we are as Christians. It is also important to note, by focusing on him first, we naturally build faith and confidence for the remaining portions of our prayer.

Christ prayed at various times during the day while on earth. One example, he prayed early in the morning: *"very early in the morning, while it was still dark, Jesus got up, left the house and went off to a solitary place, where he prayed"* (Mark 1:35 NIV).

Secondly, he prayed at night. *"Jesus went out to a mountainside to pray and spent the night praying to God"* (Luke 6:12 NIV). In this circumstance, Jesus wanted to spend time with his Father, before choosing his twelve disciples.

5

Questions:

As a group, discuss the following:

How often do each of you really pray before making an important decision?

How often do you get away to a solitary place without the distractions around you? Once a month, once a week, every day?

Contemplate:

Jesus' prayer time was a sacred time to honor and talk with his Father.

Jesus' prayer times were personally viewed as a necessity.

Why the Term Fervent Prayer?

Jesus' prayer and all true praying is fervent praying. Fervent praying is in contrast with just praying words, while not taking the words seriously. That kind of praying is merely going through some ritual form or habit. The Lord's Prayer and all true prayers are fervent prayers.

Unless distinguished differently, all usages of the word prayer in this study will be considered a prayer prayed with sincerity, a genuine desire to personally connect and communicate with God.

Jesus explained the contrast between praying with and without true sincerity in Matthew 6:5,7 NLT when he said: *"When you pray, don't be like the hypocrites who love to pray publicly where everyone can see them. I tell you the truth, that is all the reward they will get. But when you pray, don't babble on and on as the Gentiles do. They think their prayers are answered merely by repeating their words again and again."* These two Scriptural passages let us know, praying for public recognition or feeling good about oneself by verbalizing insincere words, is not fervent and genuine praying.

Being in the pastorate for many years, I have heard people pray on many occasions. I have sensed the way people pray shows how often they pray on a regular basis. One of the most memorable prayers came from a man in his late 20's who had a master's degree and a church background. He had been attending the church I pastored, and we met for lunch one day. Before we ate, I asked him if he would like to pray for our meal. He said he would, and his prayer with like this:

God is good.
God is great.
Let's us thank Him for our food.
By His hands we all are fed.
Give us Lord our daily bread.
Amen.

We continued with our meal and had a great conversation. As I left, I thought about his prayer and realized his lack of personal connection with the heavenly Father. I learned to pray from listening to my parents pray. They taught me how to pray, and I left feeling sad that no one had shown this man how to pray to the One who wanted to talk with him.

So many people today are like this young man – going through recited prayers that were learned at an early age. At some point, those prayers need to be left behind. They need to be replaced with words that communicate the warmth of our relationship with God.

Question:

Can you describe how you have experienced the difference between empty words of prayer and fervent praying in your own life?

Contemplate:

We must continually guard our prayer life and not fall into a trap of using meaningless words. God wants us to be focused and sincere when we pray.

Benefits from a Life of Fervent Prayer

Our call to fervent prayer is not just for special times that we set aside for prayer. Fervent prayer is to be continued on throughout the day. Paul tells us in 1 Thessalonians 5:17 NIV that we should *"pray continually."* To pray continually is to live in an atmosphere of constant fellowship with God; beyond one set time of praying daily.

The benefits of praying daily are too numerous to list. It is important to remember, those who do not have habits of daily prayer experience limited benefits. God wants us to live in an expectant attitude of prayer, always ready for communications from him. This is important because the Holy Spirit is continually guiding us toward blessings and warning us of spiritual dangers. Such promptings are precious privileges available for all God's children.

Here are some benefits to those who live a life of fervent prayer:

1) Praying with true sincerity opens the lines of communication with God so we can continually be in his presence. *"Then you will call upon me and come and pray to me, and I will listen to you"* (Jeremiah 29:12 NIV).

2) God is nearer to us when we pray. Deuteronomy 4:7 NIV says, *"What other nation is so great as to have their gods near them the way the Lord our God is near us whenever we pray to him?"*

3) This kind of praying delights and pleases our heavenly Father. He desires to commune with us. *"The prayer of the upright pleases him"* (Proverbs 15:8b NIV).

4) Fervent praying fortifies us in many ways to daily do the will of God. *"The prayer of a righteous person is powerful and effective"* (James 5:16b NIV).

5) Fervent praying is critical if our faith will continue to grow and develop. *"For we live by faith, not by sight"* (2 Corinthians 5:7 NIV).

Questions:

What benefits would you add to those above that you have experienced in your prayer life?

Is your life different from those who do not pray with true sincerity? Please rate it as: very much, somewhat, not much better, not at all.

How well are you receiving the benefits of fervent praying? Please rate: very well, somewhat, sometimes, rarely.

What would it take for you to receive more benefits from praying fervently?

After you have your daily prayer time, what benefits might God receive from your time with him?

Contemplate:

Benefits do not come from our good works. We cannot earn them, but all that we need will be provided as we respond to God's "if-then" proposition found in Jeremiah 29:12 NIV, *"Then you will call upon me and come and pray to me, and I will listen to you"*.

As we close this lesson, remember that prayer is not just a time to tell God what we want, it is a time to tell him we want and desire to be with him, to listen to him, and to learn from him. Prayer must be sincere if it is to be considered fervent prayer.

In our next lesson, we will be sharing three examples of fervent prayer.

A Blessing For You

May Jehovah God be with you this week!
May he bless you!
May you feel him wherever you go!

And may you give him quality time this week,
not your leftover time.

Because he gives us his best –
give him your best as well!

Lesson 2

Examples of Fervent Prayer

Before we begin our lesson, let's pray "The Lord's Prayer" together:

Our Father which art in heaven,
Hallowed be thy name.
Thy kingdom come,
Thy will be done
in earth, as it is in heaven.
Give us this day our daily bread.
And forgive us our debts,
As we forgive our debtors.
And lead us not into temptation,
but deliver us from evil:
For thine is the kingdom,
and the power, and the glory, forever.
Amen."
(Matthew 6:9-13 KJV)

In our last session we distinguished between praying some empty or spiritless form of prayer and praying a fervent prayer. We also gave an overview of what fervent prayer is and how to begin our prayer times with ascribing to God the honor he deserves. Prayer is not just giving God a list of our wants; it is spending concentrated time with him as well as living with an attitude of prayer throughout the day. Fervent prayer opens us to God's benefits and blessings that would not otherwise be received.

In this session we are going to share examples of fervent prayer. Depending on the size of the group studying this lesson, the group leader is asked to choose one or more discussion questions to use within each section.

The Lord's Prayer is a fervent prayer when we pray the prayer with an attitude of submission and respect. The Lord's Prayer represents all areas of our needs -- our daily nourishments, forgiving our debts (trespasses/sins), forgiving our debtors (those who trespass/sin against us), strength to resist temptation, and the promise of delivering us from the evil one.

Behind the beauty of this prayer is knowing our heavenly Father is watching over us as we pray daily for his will to be done in our lives. Also, to truly honor him we will strive to bring God's kingdom to this earth by our daily obedience. Fervent prayer requires more than mere repetition. It calls us to total submission to him, the one who deserves to be hallowed and revered.

Questions:

How was your prayer time this past week? What, if any, changes did you make in your time with God?

Which of the attributes or characteristics of God mentioned in our last session had greater meaning to you, and why?

At times fervent prayers can be difficult to pray. An example would be if, while we are praying, we become aware God wants us to do something that is contrary to our desires. When this happens, if we ignore God's will and try to keep on praying, our prayer ceases to be a fervent prayer because we are choosing to resist God's will.

Let's look at three biblical examples of people who prayed fervently and sought God's will rather than their own will.

Story of Hannah – *A Mother's Prayer*

Every year I would attend Vacation Bible School. I always liked the stories. One particular year, the teacher told the story of Hannah fervently praying to God because she could not give birth to a child. The story is found in 1 Samuel 1:1-2:21 NIV. Year after year, Hannah would travel to Shiloh and sacrifice to the Lord at the Tabernacle. One year she prayed:

"O Lord Almighty, if you will only look upon your servant's misery and remember me, and not forget your servant but give her a son, then I will give him to the Lord for all the days of his life, and no razor will ever be used on his head" (1 Samuel 1:11 NIV).

I remember thinking about that prayer, especially the part where she was willing to give her son back to the Lord. That made me think seriously about how I pray my prayers. Fervently praying is serious and does not regard God's will lightly. Hannah was serious in her prayer and in her promise to God.

Question:

Would you have prayed Hannah's prayer, knowing you would have to give your child back to God?

A vow is something that should not be broken. Hannah was aware of this as she brought her request to God. She carefully considered her vow and was willing to follow through on the promise she made. She respected God's will and decided to leave the answer of her having a child with him. She did not demand to have her way, but expressed her desires, respecting his wisdom and purpose. In God's time, Hannah had a baby boy who she named Samuel.

After Samuel was weaned, Hannah brought him to the Tabernacle and left him in the care of Eli the priest. What a heart-wrenching time that had to be for her, as one step of faith followed another. This was her first and only child and she had prayed countless times for his birth. Her obedience revealed the level of trust she had in God. God, in turn, honored her vow backed by obedience. The Bible records the many blessings that would come to and through Samuel.

God answered Hannah's prayer, not only by giving her a son, but also providing for him and giving him a future. Furthermore, God blessed Hannah with three more sons and two daughters (I Samuel 2:2 NLT). It is good for us to remember that God brings many unexpected blessings to those who honor him with fervent prayers and obedience.

Questions:

Give an example of someone you may know that prayed a fervent prayer for a particular request and, after a long period of time, the prayer was answered.

How might people feel while they are waiting on God?

How might a person's life change or be affected while they wait for a prayer to be answered.

Contemplate:

When waiting on God to answer our prayers, "waiting time is not wasted time." God may be preparing others on our behalf, preparing us for what is to take place, building us up in character to utilize his new gift, developing our patience, etc.

Hannah, who previously could not have a child, gave up her only son, but then God gifted her with three more sons and two daughters. God always out gives our giving!

Story of Elijah – *A Prophet's Prayer*

Elijah's name is derived from a Hebrew phrase that means "Jehovah is my God." He is another example of a fervent pray-er. When we think of the stories in the Bible about Elijah, we remember that he was fed by ravens (1 Kings 17:2-6 NIV); he went to a widow's home and prayed that her oil and flour would not run out, and later he raised her son back to life (1 Kings 17:7-24 NIV). Then, there was the time he faced the prophets of Baal at Mount Carmel (I Kings 18:16-46 NIV).

Elijah had obviously influenced the life of James in 5:17-18 NIV. James reminds us of Elijah's humanness. For someone to be so much like the rest of us, and still perform such great miracles (16 in all), James contributed all of it to Elijah's fervent praying. James also indicates that at the heart of fervent praying is based upon having a heart for righteousness.

There were times of discouragement in Elijah's life, yet he did not give up on God. God told Elijah that the rain would come. Because of the times he had spent praying, he knew God would bring the rain. He did not give up or lose hope. He trusted God to do what he said he would do. And God came through.

There was a specific time when Elijah seemingly became overwhelmed with fatigue and discouragement. It was then, while in the wilderness, he came to a broom tree, sat down under it and prayed that he might die. He told the Lord he had had enough. He asked the Lord to take his life because he was no better than his ancestors who were already dead (I Kings 19: 4b NIV).

Question:

Does becoming so tired and overwhelmed like Elijah sound familiar to you? Have you ever been in a situation like that? Share.

Contemplate:

It is wise to never make a major decision when you are emotionally and physically exhausted.

Let's continue. *"Then he (Elijah) lay down under the tree and fell asleep"* (1 Kings 19:5 NIV). This is great advice for each of us. When we have gone through a stressful time, when we have fervently prayed for an answer to something we are struggling with and feel exhausted, one of the best things we can do is to get some rest.

Getting some sleep is a great rejuvenating process God blesses today. From time to time we all need to feel rejuvenated physically, mentally, emotionally, and spiritually. When you are down, don't think God is finished with your spiritual influence and life. And once again, never make a big decision when you are depressed. Wait until after God takes you through a rejuvenating process, when you can think clearly and prayerfully consider the options.

Question:

Share a time in your life when God led you through a rejuvenating process.

An angel touched Elijah and told him to get up and eat. When he awakened, there was bread and a jar of water for him. He ate some bread, drank some water, and went back to sleep. The angel touched Elijah again and told him to get up and eat because, if he did not, the journey he was going on would be too much for him. *"So he got up and ate and drank. Strengthened by that food, he traveled forty days and forty nights until he reached Horeb, the mountain of God"* (1 Kings 19: 8 NIV).

Question:

When you have been overwhelmed in life, has God ever spoken to you by his angel or by some other means, directly or indirectly? How did God communicate to you? Describe your feeling?

It's interesting that God sent Elijah to Mount Sinai, the place where Moses met with God when God gave him the Ten Commandments. While there, Elijah told God that the people of Israel had killed all the prophets. God informed him, *"Yet I reserve 7000 in Israel – all whose knees have not bowed down to Baal and all whose mouths have not kissed him"* (1 Kings 19:18 NIV).

Elijah overcame many challenges throughout his life. Those victories can be viewed as a result of him fervently praying to and waiting for God. Let's fast forward to the New Testament when Jesus was transfigured on the mountain and Moses and Elijah appeared with him. It is said that Moses represented the law; Elijah represented the prophets; and Jesus was instituting a new covenant to bring fulfillment to both the law and the prophets.

Question:

Elijah represented the prophets when he appeared on the mountain. When you think about your spiritual influence, who would you represent most?

James wrote, *"The prayer of a righteous person is powerful and effective"* (James 5:16b NIV). The fact is, when we fervently pray, our prayers too can become like Elijah's – powerful and effective!

Question:

Who has influenced your life by the way they prayed, the results of their prayers, or their prayerful expectations, believing that what they prayed for would take place?

Contemplate:

People may never see you pray, but they will see if you have prayed by the result of your prayers.

Let's look at another time when a fervent prayer was answered. This time, someone was rescued because of the *prayers of the church.* Fervent prayers should always be part of the purpose of every church everywhere. The reason: *they work!*

Story of Peter – *A Church's Prayer*

Read the story together in Acts 12:1-17.

King Herod was arresting those who belonged to the Church to persecute them. James, the brother of John, was killed. Peter was arrested and in prison, and four squads of four soldiers each guarded him. That is sixteen soldiers guarded Peter, probably in shifts, one squad for each watch of the night.

Jesus had warned the disciples they would be imprisoned and Acts 12 talks about the third time Peter was arrested.

The first time he was arrested when he and John were speaking to the people in Acts 4:1-22 (NIV). They were brought before the rulers, the elders and the teachers of the law who were meeting in Jerusalem. There, they were *"commanded not to speak or teach at all in the name of Jesus"* (Acts 4:18 NIV). However, because the rulers feared punishing them might cause a riot, so they let them go.

The second time the apostles were arrested and put in the public jail, is recorded in Acts 5:17-40 (NIV). During the night *"an angel of the Lord opened the doors of the jail and brought them out"* (Acts 5:19 NIV). When the Sanhedrin met, it was a Pharisee named Gamaliel who addressed them and said, *"Leave these men alone! Let them go! For if their purpose of activity is of human origin, it will fail. But if it is from God, you will not be able to stop these men; you will only find yourselves fighting against God"* (Acts 5:38b-39 NIV).

Question:

If you had been arrested twice for speaking/preaching about what God had done for you, and was warned again not to continue, what might it take for you to speak out again?

Let's get back to our story of Peter's escape from prison. This time the whole Church becomes involved, not just one or two people. As the whole Church comes together and earnestly prays, notice what happens.

Peter was *"sleeping between two soldiers, bound with two chains, and sentries stood guard at the entrance"* (Acts 12:6 NIV). An angel appeared and told Peter to get up and follow him. They *"passed the first and second guards and came to the iron gate leading to the city. It opened for them by itself, and they went through it. When they had walked the length of one street, suddenly the angel left him"* (Acts 12:10 NIV).

The church was praying – Peter was sleeping – an angel wakes Peter up and takes him out of prison – the angel disappears – Peter goes to *"the house of Mary the mother of John, also called Mark, where many people had gathered and were praying"* (Acts 12:12b NIV).

This is what can happen when a church gathers to fervently pray about an urgent situation. God loves to see his children come together and ask Him to answer their prayer. He loves to see their fervency – He loves to see they are united in purpose.

Notice, while all this was happening, the Church was praying!

Questions:

Name one or more times when your church prayed fervently about a special need in the church or the community. What was the outcome?

Did it strengthen your faith and prayer life? Share your answer.

Contemplate:

We need to have churches that become spiritually burdened and are led by the Spirit to pray, just as we need individuals to be led by the Spirit to pray.

Someone in the Church started that prayer meeting for Peter. Perhaps the most important thing God wants you to do today is to start or participate in a church prayer meeting.

As we close our time together in this lesson, remember this: even if you never see the answers to your prayers in your lifetime, never, never, never give up on praying fervently. Praying fervently always changes the situation, changes you, or changes both.

The mother's prayer of Hannah represents those who have prayed for years for a particular request and were willing to modify her desires by putting God's will before their own.

Elijah's ability to pray with power and for great miracles did not keep him from experiencing human emotions and depression.

If two or three gathered in fervent prayer can open prison doors, think about what your church can do in concerted fervent prayer!

There are more biblical stories to exemplify fervent prayer, but more importantly are the examples you and I will provide to those who are looking to us for inspiration and guidance.

*   *   *   *   *   *   *

If your group enjoys singing, close this time together by singing this hymn of the church, *"Near to the Heart of God."* If your group would prefer to read the words of the song in unison, feel free to do so while considering the meaning of its words.

Near to the Heart of God

There is a place of quiet rest,
near to the heart of God;
A place where sin cannot molest,
near to the heart of God.

Refrain:
O Jesus, blest Redeemer,
sent from the heart of God;
Hold us, who wait before Thee,
near to the heart of God.
There is a place of comfort sweet,
near to the heart of God;
A place where we our Savior meet,
near to the heart of God.

There is a place of full release,
near to the heart of God;
A place where all is joy and peace,
near to the heart of God.

17

Lesson 3

Personal Prayer Prints

Scriptures:

"But be sure that everything is done properly and in order" (I Corinthians 14:40 NLT).

"When you pray, don't babble on and on [praying without understanding] as the Gentiles do. They think their prayers are answered merely by repeating their words again and again" (Matthew 6:7 NLT).

"we don't know what God wants us to pray for" (Romans 8:26b NLT).

Sir Frances Galton, an anthropologist, was a pioneer in fingerprint identification. He was the first person to prove scientifically that people could be identified by their fingerprints. Such uniqueness can also be seen in our prayer lives. Everyone who prays regularly prays using a different pattern. The pattern may be purposely organized or may have simply evolved over time; but all people who pray regularly, pray with some pattern whether they realize it or not.

Further, just like the friction ridges on a fingerprint are different, in that some are longer, some are shorter, and some are different in depth, so the prayer prints of our prayer list are different.

What Are Prayer Prints?

A prayer print is simply the way a person prays. It is a conscious or subconscious way we express our feelings or needs to God. All who pray with fervency and sincerity have a personalized prayer print which assists them in praying.

When our kids were young, we taught them to pray before going to sleep. I would tell them what to say and then they would repeat what I had said. Each night the wording may have been different, but the following is one example of words we used:

"Thank You, God, for this day you have given us. Thank you for being with us and keeping us safe. Thank you for our family (we would list the names of those within our immediate family). *Thank you for our church and for our missionaries. Give us a good night's sleep. We love you, God. Amen."*

Those are beautiful thoughts for a child. And, in its simplest form, this child's prayer can be thought of as a pattern to follow, a model or what I am calling a "prayer print". This child's prayer covers the important needs of the young child for that time. As children grow, their needs will change; and a prayer of confession will someday be needed to be added.

As we grow older and spiritually, our "prayer print" should grow. It will expand as additional people and needs are added and become smaller as prayers are answered and victories recorded. Our prayer print should adjust to our situation in life and the calling God has placed on us during that situation.

Question:

What was your earliest prayer print (the way you prayed), whether as a child or an adult?

Contemplate:

No one has a fingerprint or prayer print exactly like anyone else's. It is as unique as our relationship with God.

Prayer prints are to the spiritual body what exercise is to the human body.

What Prayer Prints Might Look Like

Personal prayer prints may vary drastically in form. The question is, what form is the most helpful to your prayer life? Let's look at this example, the one that is most helpful to me.

My Prayer Print Circle

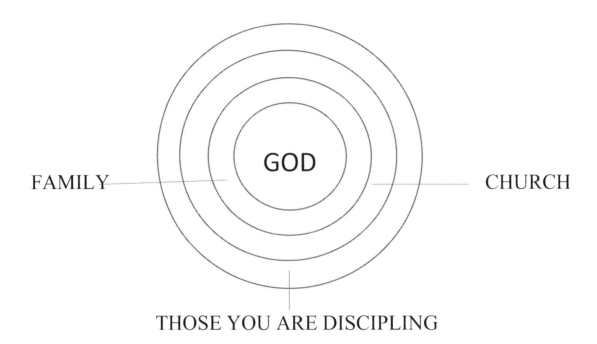

The first and inner circle is always God, and that is where we begin our prayer time as we honor and praise him for who he is and what he has done for us.

- The second circle may be where you pray for your spouse and family.

- The third circle could include the needs of your church and specific individuals in the church.

- The fourth circle could be those you are discipling or influencing for Christ. This circle could include long term prayer needs that may take months or years.

You could continue with another circle for your own personal spiritual challenges and needs. As needed, other circles could be added for unusual prayer requests that come from time to time. The order of these circles can be changed or personalized as needed. Prayer prints are meant to be changed.

If you choose to use a list as a prayer print, your print may look something like this:

My Prayer Print List
God
Spouse
Children & grandchildren
Family members

Church
Those I am discipling
Personal challenges.

You may want to have more than one prayer print list -- family members on one list, church needs on another, and your spiritual and personal challenges on a third.

Note:

If you are using a prayer print list, it is easier to remember each list if they are shorter.

Discussion:

Without mentioning any names or personal prayer requests, draw a diagram of what your prayer print looks like, or share with the group how you progress through your time in prayer.

Question:

Specifically, what did you learn from the prayer prints of others in the group?

Prayer prints can change over time.

Differing from fingerprints, prayer prints can evolve and form new shapes over time. They will change as prayer requests grow or diminish. They can begin in one shape and evolve into another or add an additional separate diagram or list. The possibilities are endless depending on the creativity and needs of the one praying. The absolute key question is "What's an easy pattern or print for you to remember as you pray?" Whatever model you choose does not have to remain forever. You can change prayer prints as your prayers change over time.

Questions:

What was a circumstance in your life when you noticed you needed to adjust your prayer print in your daily personal time with God?

How long have you been using your present prayer print?

Contemplate:

Because God made us all different, no wonder we have different prayer prints.

Benefits to Using a Prayer Print

Nowhere in the Bible do we have a specific command to use a prayer print any more than scripture tells us what utensil to use when we eat. However, we do know that we must follow healthy eating patterns if we are going to be physically healthy. In the same manner that we give attention to our physical bodies to remain healthy, we must also give appropriate attention to our relationship with God through prayer to be healthy spiritually.

You may wonder if it is worth the time and effort to invest in a life of fervent prayer, given that we live in a world filled with so many demands on our time, not to include life's enormous complexities. The answer is yes. Our prayer life is essential if we care about benefiting from God's direction and wisdom. Spending quality time with God will help us know where to focus our efforts and use our limited resources. But, to reap the rewards of prayer, we must be serious about our commitment to communicate with God regularly. And remember, there is no real prayer life unless it is filled with sincerity, and sincerity includes having an effective prayer print. Let's look at the benefits of having a prayer print.

The following list of benefits pertain to having a primary daily prayer time. (Short prayers throughout the day are beneficial but we also need a time in which God has our full attention.) So, what are the benefits of having a primary prayer time and using a prayer print?

1. If you are interrupted, and must leave your prayer time, it is easy to come back and know where to begin again.

2. If you are tired and your mind begins to wander, or you simply become distracted, you can remember where you were in traveling through your prayer print.

3. It is easier to remember who you have prayed for and who you might have left out.

4. If you are sick and not feeling well, you can bundle (condense) your prayer in a sentence or two, hand it to God, and specifically know what you are giving to him. After all, *"God gives rest (sleep) to his loved ones"* (Psalm 127:2 NLT).

5. New requests and needs can be added to the prayer print without confusing them with other ongoing needs.

6. Having a designated place on your prayer print for personal needs allows you to have quality time with God about those needs without feeling guilty you are not praying for others.

7. You can sense when the Holy Spirit interrupts your prayer time and wants you to spend more or less time on specific needs. By his Spirit, he lets you know when to adjust the priorities within the prayer print.

8. After prayers are answered, there will be certain places along the print where you will recall the answers to prayer and rejoice in the victories again.

9. Using prayer prints as a daily spiritual exercise will foster personal spiritual growth.

10. Praying with a prayer print reminds us that we are dependent upon God every day.

11. When you have finished praying through your prayer print, you are assured you have completed your holy work of prayer.

Questions:
Which of the benefits mentioned above have you experienced?

Which ones have been most beneficial to you?

Contemplate:
How does praying to God about people help us to get to know them better?

Prayer Print Adjustments and Advice

Listen closely to the Holy Spirit about who to pray for and when to adjust your prayer focus. Some requests may need to be taken off your prayer list and new ones added.

If you tell people you will be praying for them, do so. Be careful how you tell people you will be praying for them. Being specific will help you know when your promise to pray is complete, and you can move on with other needs.

Do not let your prayer print become a sacred process that cannot be changed. Like exercise routines they need changing from time to time. Be loyal to the objective but remember that the objective is to communicate with God, not to be a servant to a system. It is only a tool to assist you to grow in your relationship with God.

Sometimes you may need to hand your burdens to God in a bundle. Then, go to sleep knowing you are in his peaceful presence. He not only has you in his safe keeping, but all your prayers and needs.

Question:

Because every day can seem to be a busy day, some people might tend to rush through their prayer needs or "bundle" their prayers too often. How often do you bundle most of your prayers?

Contemplate:

Rarely should we bundle because it can slow our spiritual growth, because we are not spending time in fellowship with God.

When should a person stop praying for a certain need? When the prayer has been answered we can stop unless the Spirit prompts us to continue to pray. We should always follow the Spirit's leading.

There are special long-term requests that we may bring to God for years, seemingly without an answer. God will give us his peace when we are to conclude our prayer efforts and leave the situation in his hands.

Prayer prints need to be constantly adjusted as we take off some needs and add others. If we never took anyone off our prayer list, a time would come when we would not have time to pray for all the new requests. Furthermore, we may lose our focus on one primary objective of prayer, personal spiritual development. Prayer prints must never become a duty to be fulfilled, but rather a sacred discipline of partnership with God.

Contemplate:

Because some of us love our routines, it may be very difficult to remove people and their requests from our prayer list.

The devil is the author of confusion, even in our prayer life.

Closing:

Remember, like fingerprints, all prayer prints are different. Every person who prays regularly has a prayer print. Prayer prints may change according to circumstances and the leading of the Spirit. Prayer prints, infused with fervent praying, provide great benefits.

Close in prayer while thanking God for our uniqueness in how we pray, and for God's ability to hear and understand every prayer.

Lesson 4

Four Attitudes for Fervent Praying

Psalm 23:1-6 NIV

"The Lord is my shepherd, I shall not be in want.
He makes me lie down in green pastures,
he leads me beside quiet waters, he restores my soul.
He guides me in paths of righteousness for his name's sake.
Even though I walk through the valley of the shadow of death,
I will fear no evil, for you are with me;
your rod and your staff, they comfort me.
You prepare a table before me in the presence of my enemies.
You anoint my head with oil; my cup overflows.
Surely goodness and love will follow me all the days of my life,
And I will dwell in the house of the Lord forever.

As we talked about in Lesson 1, fervent prayer is having a sincere conversation with God. In Lesson 2, we recognized three Biblical characters who were great examples of fervent prayer. In Lesson 3 we considered just how we can create our own prayer prints. Like fingerprints, our approaches may be different, but the objective is the same, to grow in our relationship with God. We further explained that prayer prints are organized ways we approach God in prayer.

In this lesson, we are going to share another way to pray fervently. The four parts of this lesson can be used as a guide for a prayer print and are essential attitudes for anyone who approaches God with sincerity.

This lesson has been organized in the simple acronym P.R.A.Y. This acronym came to me some time back. I have also used it as a prayer print and in combination with the list prayer print. Most importantly, each letter of the acronym P.R.A.Y must be central to our attitude when we pray. Our attitudes must be filled with Praise, Restoration, Adoration and Yearning. As these four attitudes are presented, we will be considering David's prayer, Psalm 23. Let's begin with the first letter "P".

Praise, Restoration, Adoration, & Yearning

P – Praise

Praise is our attempt to express deep gratitude for all He has done. To praise is to say "thank you" to God. When we praise God, we show him honor and respect. We know from scripture that all creation praises God. This includes the angels in Heaven as well as the lower forms of His creation.

> *"Praise the Lord, you angels, you mighty ones who carry out his plans, listening for each of his commands. Praise the Lord, everything he has created, everything in all his kingdom. Let all that I am praise the Lord"* (Psalm 103:20, 22 NLT).

There are other Scriptures where praise is shared directly and indirectly. One passage that boldly communicates praise for God is David's twenty-third Psalm. We read in Psalm 23:1-2 NIV:

> *"The Lord is my shepherd, I shall not be in want.*
> *He makes me lie down in green pastures,*
> *He leads me beside quiet waters…"*

In the first verse, David strongly but indirectly praised God with the words, "I shall not be in want". As a lad, David began his life's work as a shepherd boy and later rose to be king of his nation. As king, he had all the power and money that he needed. But in his mind, he lacked something, and that led to his temptation and sin. As an older man, David realizes, because of having God as his Great Shepherd, he did not need anything. God took take care of him. To the degree we lack gratitude for God's gifts is the degree we are headed toward sin.

David no doubt remembered that he, as a good shepherd, provided for his sheep. When they were hungry, he led them to green pastures. He knew that when the sheep were hungry, they stood, and when they were full and satisfied, they laid down. When the waters were turbulent, the sheep were frightened, so David would find quiet waters for his sheep   Now, when he looks back on his life, he sees how God led him to both green pastures and quiet waters. David praises God for always providing for him.

Here are a few Scriptures to help us initiate our praise.

> *"Always by joyful. Never stop praying. Be thankful in all circumstances, for this is God's will for you who belong to Christ Jesus"* (I Thessalonians 5:16-18 NLT).

> *"And we know that God causes everything to work together for the good of those who love God and are called according to His purpose for them"* (Romans 8:28 NLT).

> *"Therefore, let us offer through Jesus a continual sacrifice of praise to God, proclaiming our allegiance to his name"* (Hebrews 13:15 NLT).

Questions:

In Psalm 23, David praises God indirectly when he uses the phrase, *"I shall not be in want."* What phrase might you use as you refer to your unknown future?

Some people do not give out many words of appreciation throughout the day. They may withhold words of praise to a waiter while eating in a restaurant, or to a cashier who needs cheering up. Why do you think that is the case?

Why do some people find it difficult to take time to praise God in their daily prayer times?

Where does giving God praise occur in your daily prayer time? Does it occur at the beginning of the prayer, the middle, the end, and why?

When was the last time you expressed thanks (praise) to someone in the church by sharing with them how God had blessed you through them?

Contemplate:

A lack of gratitude is at a root of sin. To the degree we lack spiritual gratitude we are moving toward sinfulness (Romans 1:21 NIV).

We should not only give praise to God in our private prayer times, we should also praise people in the church when God uses them to bless us.

Praise, or having a thankful attitude, should be part of every fervent and sincere prayer.

The second attitude that should be in our prayers is a desire to be restored spiritually.

R – Restoration

Having an attitude that desires spiritual restoration is an attitude of submission to God. When we pray for restoration, we are always seeking a better life.

The idea of restoration is found throughout Scripture, especially from the time of the prophets to the time of Jesus. Jesus is viewed as the continual restorer, moving His followers toward what He called "the way, the truth, and the life."

When we sincerely want to have a better relationship with God, we are seeking some form of restoration. This can be for the forgiveness of sin, for purity that comes through sanctification, or growing in Christlikeness.

The good news is, when we are willing, God is able to restore us. God's restoring of David has become an encouraging hope for many people. In Psalm 23:3-4 NIV, we read,

"he restores my soul.
He guides me in paths of righteousness for his name's sake.
Even though I walk through the valley of the shadow of death,
I will fear no evil, for you are with me;
your rod and your staff, they comfort me.

As we read Psalm 23:3-4, David testifies that he had been and was still being restored. David had sinned and sought forgiveness (Ps. 51:1 NIV). He had also asked God to create a clean heart within him (Ps. 51:10 NIV). The truth is, all of us have sinned and come short of the glory of God (Romans 3:23 NIV). Also, the truth is, all of us are continually being restored as we grow spiritually.

Like David, our journey to restoration may not be immediate. Some restorations take a long time. Saul's intent was to kill David, but God protected him and used the wilderness to prepare him for Israel's throne. God used all David's years in the wilderness to prepare him for leadership.

The rod or staff of the shepherd was used to guard the sheep from animals that would attack. The same rod was used to correct the young sheep as they might try to go astray. Likewise, the rod or staff of the Great Shepherd protected David from Saul. The staff was used to protect David from himself, in giving him wisdom not to kill Saul. The staff of the Great Shepherd provided lessons in leadership and comfort to David as he escaped Saul attempts on his life.

Once again, all this took place over a matter of years while God was restoring David to new levels of leadership and higher levels of character. David simply said, "he restores my soul" (23:3 NIV).

Contemplate:
An attitude of restoration requires submission to God's will.

David sought God's approval. Saul sought the approval of those around him.

We need to be restored from our sins, but also to know what God's purpose is for us.

We are all in the process of being restored to the Image of Christ.

Here are some other Scriptures to meditate on as we experience restoration.

> *"For the time is coming when I will restore the fortunes of my people of Israel and Judah. I will bring them home to this land that I gave to their ancestors, and they will possess it again. I, the Lord, have spoken"* (Jeremiah 30:3 NLT).

> *"'I have seen what they do, but I will heal them anyway! I will lead them. I will comfort those who mourn, bringing words of praise to their lips. May they have abundant peace, both near and far,' says the Lord, who heals them"* (Isaiah 57:18-19 NLT).

> *"In his kindness God called you to share in his eternal glory by means of Christ Jesus. So after you have suffered a little while, he will restore, support, and strengthen you, and he will place you on a firm foundation. All power to him forever! Amen"* (I Peter 510-11 NLT).

Questions:

How have you sought restoration in your prayer life? Remember: we must seek restoration with submissiveness, and we are always seeking restoration for a better spiritual life.

In what ways have you been involved in restoring others who have strayed from a Christlike life? Like a shepherd, did you need to use a rod to nudge or a staff to comfort?

Describe what it feels like to realize you, too, need some form of restoration?

An attitude of adoration is also critical in our prayer lives.

A – Adoration

When we adore God, we are captivated by some area of His greatness. We are fascinated by Him, perhaps about how He does things. Simply put, adoration is experiencing a moment of "awe" and "deep love" as God draws our attention. Every prayer time does not have to have something spectacular to take place, but, when we come to prayer, our attitude should include an awareness of our love for God and our being fascinated with Him.

Adoration is different from praise. Adoration is experienced internally as the presence of God is acknowledged and personally enjoyed. Adoration can also be experienced and expressed externally as we lift hands in the air. When experiencing adoration internally, the worshiper may not want to move physically or even speak because of the sacredness of the moment. When experienced both internally and externally, some may desire to shout out God's praise, while feeling if they don't, the rocks may cry out.

To talk about adoration in the context of a public worship service is important for this lesson because, when we practice adoration in our prayer times, we are preparing for adoration in public worship.

True adoration cannot be humanly manipulated or emotionally manufactured. Adoration is an awareness of God's presence, and a deep appreciation for His wonderous works.

In Psalm 23:5 NIV we read,

"You prepare a table before me in the presence of my enemies.
You anoint my head with oil; my cup overflows."

I believe David was fascinated and in awe of what God was doing. David was in prayer and thinking about God preparing a table for him. Can you imagine what it might be like to realize God was going to honor you personally? In that day, when you entered a house, the host would anoint you with oil. David was envisioning that God was the host, and that He was going to honor a shepherd boy. The cup represented how he took take care of David and protected him. God had protected and taken care of David down through the years. Not only did he provide for David, but He also restored his soul. Why did God restore David soul? It was because he had something else for David to do. And yes, He has something else for you to do as well.

David's cup is overflowing with blessings. This cup represents the caring aspect of God. It also represents David's weaknesses in being human. We can try to keep our cup full of spiritual disciplines, but only God can overflow it. God overflowing us with strength and blessings is how God's new task will be accomplished.

When David was writing this Psalm, he looked back over the years at the paths he had traveled and marveled that, after his failings, God would restore him for a new spiritual assignment. David was captivated by God's mercy, and he was fascinated by God's love. He was looking at his God with overwhelming adoration.

Contemplate:

God wants to anoint my head with oil in my prayer times.

The presence of my enemies can include my temptations and spiritual weaknesses.

Restoration always leads to adoration.

Here are some Scriptures to reflect the joy of adoration.

"You are worthy, O Lord our God, to receive glory and honor and power. For you created all things, and they exist because you created what you pleased" (Revelation 4:11 NLT).

"But as for me, I will sing about your power. Each morning I will sing with joy about your unfailing love. For you have been my refuge, a place of safety when I am in distress" (Psalm 59:16 NLT).

"My old self has been crucified with Christ. It is no longer I who live, but Christ lives in me. So, I live in this earthly body by trusting in the Son of God, who loved me and gave himself for me" (Galatians 2:20 NLT).

"For God is Spirit, so those who worship him must worship in spirit and in truth" (John 4:24 NLT).

Questions:

What is the difference in practicing adoration in private worship in contrast to the public worship with other believers?

To experience adoration is not as easy as turning on a light switch. It may take time to unwind from the daily cares before our spiritual sensitivities become more alert. How often do you experience adoration in your devotional life?

Make a list of several thoughts that you can meditate on to assist you toward moments of adoration.

Yearning is our fourth attitude as we penetrate the heavens.

Y – Yearning

To yearn is to long for or strongly desire for something. We should yearn or long for God's will over our own desires. The devil tries to get us to give our attention to something. Then he wants us to yearn for it. Whatever we yearn for ultimately defines our life. God wants us to yearn for Him because He knows what will make us happy eternally. Many people may have Biblical knowledge and a church background, but they will never be satisfied spiritually without yearning for God to be active in their lives.

David was yearning before God when he prayed, *"Create in me a pure heart, O God, and renew a steadfast spirit within me"* (Psalm 51:10 NIV).

David was also yearning for God's continued presence when we read in Psalm 23:6 NIV:
"Surely goodness and love will follow me all the days of my life,
And I will dwell in the house of the Lord forever."

Yearning for God can be experienced as a spiritual emptiness, being lonely for His presence, or a desire to prioritize our schedules so we can be with God. Yearning is something that must be pursued if it is to grow. Feeding our yearning for God involves spending time in prayer, reading and adjusting our lives to His Word, receiving His leading as we worship with others, etc. If we are to yearn for God, we must separate ourselves from those things that smothers the peace he gives and tarnishes our witness.

God desires that a nonbeliever, as well as saints, yearn for Him. It is the only way we can experience his continual blessings. David's goal was to yearn for God all his life. David believed that, after a life of yearning, he could look back and see God's goodness and love had followed him every day of his life. When we feed our yearning for God and starve any yearning that does not please Him, His Spirit will bear witness with our spirits that He is with us.

David began yearning for God as a young lad caring for his father's sheep. David was described in the Scriptures as a man after God's own heart. David never yearned to fulfill rules or legalistic traditions. He wanted to act, think, and feel the way God did. This longing took him through many trials and persecutions to test his faith and strain his self-control.

Scripture reveals that David failed at times and needed to repent and begin again. But he never stopped desiring to be like His heavenly Father and obey Him. Because he never stopped yearning for God, he could write songs and poems about his experiences and share about the goodness and mercy of God. David looked back on his life and said, *"Taste and see that the Lord is good; blessed is the man who takes refuge in Him"* (Psalm 34: 8, NIV). David had experienced the inner torment that comes from the wages of sin, but also the gift of God's eternal life. David continued to yearn for God throughout his life. He realized the taste of Godliness was far more alluring than any yearning for evil that Satan might bring.

This prayer of David in Psalm 23:1-6 gives us a picture of God's protection and His determination to guide and direct. More than that, it is the story about a weak sheep, named David, who yearned to follow his Great Shepherd.

Contemplate:

David's yearning reached beyond this life to dwelling in the house of the Lord.

Sometimes a kid wants to be like his dad who drives a car. Sometimes a shepherd boy wants to be like "the One" who made the stars.

Scriptures:

"Search for the Lord and for his strength; continually seek him" (I Chronicles 16:11 NLT).

"I long, yes, I faint with longing to enter the courts of the Lord" (Psalm 84:2a NLT).

"Like newborn babies, you must crave pure spiritual milk so that you will grow into a full experience of salvation. Cry out for this nourishment, now that you have had a taste of the Lord's kindness" (I Peter 2:2-3 NLT).

"When the Spirit of truth comes, he will guide you into all truth" (John 16:13a NLT).

"Whom have I in heaven but you? I desire you more than anything on earth" (Psalm 73:25 NLT).

"You can ask for anything in my name, and I will do it, so that the Son can bring glory to the Father. Yes, ask me for anything in my name, and I will do it" (John 14:13-14 NLT)!

"Now I will rise up to rescue them, as they have longed for me to do" (Psalm 12: 5b NLT).

Questions:

Describe the difference in two people who are in love yearning to be with one another and someone yearning to be with God? What are the similarities and differences?

Why do people yearn to be with God?

How do you think God responds differently to people who yearn to be with him and those who don't?

In this lesson we have considered four attitudes that must be at the center of our praying. We have especially considered David and his sincerity of heart as he fervently prayed. In our next lesson we will be studying the life and actions of three great pray-ers in the Bible.

Close with prayer. In addition to the present needs, pray that God will help all of us to be more sensitive to our attitudes when we pray.

Lesson 5

When God Says NO to a Prayer

It has been said that God answers all prayers. The answers are yes, no, or wait a while. Obviously, we have very little problem when the answer is "yes". However, we tend to struggle when God's answer is "wait a while". The answer "no" can almost be overwhelming, and yet it can be the greatest place for our faith to grow.

When my wife was seven years old, her mother died of cancer. She told me that when they received the news early in the morning, she started praying to God to bring her mom back to life. After all, God brought people back to life in the Bible and, if he did it then, he could do it again. She was sincere in her prayer and waited patiently for him to do it. She remembers going to the visitation and seeing her mom in the casket and reminding God it was not too late to bring her back to life.

The day of the funeral arrived and, as she was sitting in church during the funeral service, she once again reminded God it was not too late. She, as a seven-year-old waited patiently. The service ended and she went by the casket for the last time and saw her mother lying there. As she walked out of the church, her hopes were still strong. It wasn't until she arrived at the cemetery that she realized God was not going to answer her prayer. It was hard for her to understand why God said no.

Weeks later, she had a dream she was at church and walked outside the building. At that moment she saw her mother walking on the sidewalk toward the church. She ran out to meet her and said, "I knew He would send you back to me." Her mother quietly said, "I'm not coming back; I'm staying in heaven with Jesus, but you are going to be okay." When my wife awakened, she knew God's prayer was no, but in her seven-year-old way, she was fine with it, and she knew God loved her. She realized that God would not always answer her prayers with a "yes", but He would answer her prayers the way He thought best. This experience strengthened her in the years ahead in her prayer life, and in her devotion to her Heavenly Father. He always knew what was best for her!

In this lesson, we will consider three Biblical characters who experienced God saying "no" to their prayers. They are Abraham, Jesus, and Paul. We will begin with **Abraham**.

Scripture:

"And Abraham said to God, 'if only Ishmael might live under your blessing!"
(Genesis 17:18 NIV).

Abraham

"The Last Dance" was shown as an ESPN Documentary directed by Jason Heir. The documentary showed a crucial time in the game when Karl Malone needed to make two free throws to help win the game. He was a good 74% shooter from the line. With the tension and the crowd on edge, Malone was about to get set at the line when Scotty Pippen, on the opposing team, walked over a few steps and said to him, "the mailman doesn't deliver on Sunday." Malone was known as "the mailman" and it was Sunday. Following those words, this great player missed both free throws and Michael Jordon, who played for the opposing team, made the final shot that won the game.

Great basketball players have failed and great followers of God have also failed. To say the least, Abraham was one of the greatest examples of someone exercising faith in the Old Testament. But when God stepped over to Abraham and told him he would have a son, he seemingly lost his poise. Let's review Abraham's journey.

God had told Abraham years before that He was going to provide Abraham with a son. However, Abraham became impatient when a son did not come, and decided to do God's work for him. He had a son by one of his servant girls to help God out. Now, it is thirteen years later. God is not only following through on His original promise; God is also changing Abraham's plans that he had worked out in detail. Ishmael was thirteen years old now and, over these years, Abraham had gotten close to this young lad. Ishmael had walked alongside Abraham, and they had shared a special life together. It seemed all of Abraham plans were flawless until God approached Abraham about Isaac, who was God's choice to fulfill his purpose.

Abraham responded to God by saying, *"if only Ishmael might live under your blessing"* (Genesis 17:18 NIV). As far as Abraham was concerned, he did not need Isaac when his son Ishmael could do whatever God needed. Besides, he already knew Ishmael. What if Isaac disturbed their comfortable relationship and routines. Abraham, this man of prayer and mighty in faith, found it hard to believe God had a better plan than his own.

Abraham's prayer and desire was for Ishmael to be God's chosen representative, not Isaac. But God did not listen to Abraham's advice, his wishes, nor was he sensitive to the emotional attachment that Abraham and Ishmael had cultivated. Abraham had presumed on God. Abraham had worked out his own plan and assumed God would agree to it. Abraham may have reasoned, "You owe me given all I have done and sacrificed in following you." He could have tried to sell God on the fact that all the planning was for God's glory. But God was firm. In the final analysis, if Abraham was going to continue to be a man of faith, he would have to trust God, not only with the birth of Isaac, but also with his relationship with Ishmael.

Abraham chose to follow God's plan, and later saw that God's plan was superior to his own.

Contemplate:

Whenever we make our own plan, it is never as good as God's plan.

Just because we think our plan is anointed by God, does not mean God thinks it is.

This story shows that the closer someone is to us emotionally, mentally, etc., the harder it is not to be biased when God chooses someone else.

Abraham was a man who grew in faith, one experience at a time.

One of the greatest tests in growing in faith is when our prayers are not answered according to our asking. That is when a new deeper faith begins.

Questions:

God shared with Abraham what His will was for him. Has God ever spoken to you through a thought or a scripture which gave you specific guidance? Are you willing to share your story?

Why would you tell people they should always wait for God's answer?

Describe how you think Abraham felt while he was having this disagreement with God?

Have you ever recommended to God what you thought was a better plan, and he chose his plan over yours? How did his plan work out?

Jesus

Scripture:

"My soul is overwhelmed with sorrow to the point of death" (Matthew 26:38 NIV).

"He went away a second time and prayed, "My Father, if it is not possible for this cup to be taken away unless I drink it, may your will be done" (Matthew 26:42 NIV).

The second Bible character we are going to consider who experienced not having a prayer answered is **Jesus**. The feelings of sorrow and trouble can come rolling in as sudden as storm clouds. We may not be surprised by their coming, but we can become unnerved when they arrive.

Nowhere else in Scripture do we see Jesus' likeness to our own frailty and humanity more than in the Garden of Gethsemane. In Gethsemane we see a progression of his emotional distress as well as the progression of apathy from the disciples. Jesus began by saying he was sorrowful and troubled. Then, as with a sudden sickness, he said, *"My soul is overwhelmed with sorrow to the point of death"* (Matthew 26:38 NIV). Jesus desperately needed to be in the presence of the Father to pray. He also needed to experience true friendship. The disciples did not have to give words of encouragement but, at least, they could have stayed awake while Jesus struggled in prayer with his Father.

Jesus prayed to the Father three times during that night. Those prayers were grueling, as the repulsiveness of taking the cup was being considered. Jesus prayed, *"My Father, if it is possible, may this cup be taken away from me. Yet not as I will, but as you will"* (Matthew 26:39b NIV). His second and third prayers were the same in words but grew in intensity. *"My Father, if it is not possible for this cup to be taken away unless I drink it, may your will be done"* (Matthew 26:42 NIV). Jesus fervently prayed. His heart's cries were personal and pointed. Yet, He used phrases such as *"if it is possible"*, *"yet not as I will, but as you will"*, and *"if it is not possible, may your will be done."*

Jesus' prayer or desire was not granted as He had hoped. In that sense, His prayer was not answered. However, as Jesus submitted his human preferences, his resolve was strengthened to go forward with God's purpose. After he prayed His third prayer, He returned to the disciples. At that time, His betrayer's mob approached, and He proclaimed, *"Rise, let us go"* (Matthew 26:46 NIV).

Questions:

Do you become weak in temptation because you forget you are a child of God?

Can you share a time when God had a particular plan or purpose for you, and you went through a real spiritual struggle before you surrendered your will?

How do you think Jesus felt after He submitted His will to the Father?

Contemplate:

Jesus' attitude and behavior never wavered concerning his identity as God's Son and his mission to be obedient to the end.

The principle in 1 Corinthians 10:13 (NIV) can be applied to Jesus' life. *"And God is faithful; he will not let you be tempted beyond what you can bear. But when you are tempted, he will also provide a way out so that you can stand up under it."* Either God takes away the temptation, or He gives us strength to overcome it.

Your closest friends can never understand your spiritual challenges and burdens like you do. Only Jesus understands.

Paul

Scripture:

> *"To keep me from becoming conceited because of these surpassingly great revelations, there was given me a thorn in my flesh, a messenger of Satan, to torment me"* (II Corinthians 12:7 NIV).

The third Bible character we are going to consider in this lesson who experienced not having a particular prayer answered is **Paul**.

Have you ever thought you could better serve God today if the residue of your past was not in the way? Your past might have included a bad home environment, growing up poor and not being able to secure the right education, an ugly scar from a horrific car accident, a birth defect that limits your sight or hearing, etc.

We don't know what Paul's thorn in the flesh was, but we know it was more than a small splinter in which he could pull out and go on his way. Paul's thorn was considered overwhelming and something that would seriously prohibit his effectiveness in ministry. Paul had the right education and he studied at the feet of the renowned rabbi Gamaliel for ten years. This gave Paul high status because Gamaliel was a Jew who had a doctorate in Jewish Law. Paul was considered a moral achiever, being a Pharisee of the Pharisees. He was a true success story and seemingly had achieved most if not everything on his own.

When Paul met Christ on the Damascus Road, his life changed. It changed more, along the way, as he recognized he was limited by his thorn in the flesh. Paul prayed three times that this thorn in the flesh be removed, and for the right reason. He wanted to fulfill God's purpose. Once again, we are not told what the thorn was, but we are told that Paul struggled as he begged God three times to remove it.

Paul's prayer was not answered, in the sense the thorn was not removed. But how Paul thought about his thorn was transformed by the mighty words of Jesus in 2 Corinthians 12:9: *"My grace is sufficient for you, for my power is made perfect in weakness."* Then Paul responded, *"Therefore I will boast all the more gladly about my weaknesses, so that Christ's power may rest on me."*

Paul's new understanding of his thorn was not an ultimate hinderance in fulfilling God's purpose, but rather a divine gift to enable his ministry. He celebrated when he said, *"That is why, for Christ's sake, I delight in weaknesses, in insults, in hardships, in persecutions, in difficulties. For when I am weak, then I am strong"* (2 Corinthians 12:10 NIV).

What weaknesses, hindrances, or thorns are you celebrating today?

Questions:

What thorn might you have? If you feel comfortable, please share with the group.

If your thorn were removed, how might you and your ministry be affected?

As you consider your thorn, are you willing to see it as an advantage rather than a hinderance?

Some people may feel like they have a thorn in their life, and other people may feel they have more like a thorn tree to contend with in life. Would you be willing to accept a thorn tree if God's grace would be sufficient and His power would be perfect?

Contemplate:

God's grace is sufficient, and God's power is made perfect in weakness.

Paul was willing to change his opinion of his thorn to Jesus' opinion.

As you think about your prayer life and the prayers that have been sent up to God from you, would you be willing to say as my wife did as a seven-year-old: *"God would not always answer her prayers with a "yes", but He would answer her prayers the way He thought best."* God's best answer for us at times is "No" because he loves each one of us and knows what's best for us.

Even when God's says "No" thank him for that answer. You may never know what he has saved you from because of that answer. He truly loves you!

Closing:

Have a moment of silent prayer allowing everyone to give praise to God for the times He said "No".

Sometimes God's best yes is a "No"

Notes:

Section 2:

Compassionate Outreach

Lesson 1: Compassionate Outreach

Scripture: *"When Jesus landed and saw a large crowd, he had compassion on them, because they were like sheep without a shepherd. So he began teaching them many things"* (Mark 7:34 NIV).

Our second core principle is Compassionate Outreach. In this series of lessons, we will consider some of the basic components of Compassionate Outreach.

Lesson 1: We will distinguish the difference between empathy and compassion, Jesus' role concerning empathy and compassion, what is outreach and why it is important. Also, we will recognize some characteristics of outreach among disciples.

Lesson 2: we will see how compassionate outreach looked in the life of Jesus as He ministered to the Samaritan woman.

Lesson 3: we will highlight some suggestions and insights in sharing the Gospel. We will also discuss methods and tools for sharing the Gospel.

Lesson 4: We will reminisce over some experiences we have had concerning compassionate outreach in comparison with the experiences of Jesus and others.
Let's get started!

What is the difference in empathy and compassion?

Empathy and compassion are very similar. Yet, for this study, there is a subtle and important difference. Let us begin with empathy.

Empathy is an important part of every class and small group within a church. People sharing empathy are genuinely concerned that others do not suffer any more than necessary. They want to listen as someone in the group expresses their pain. When there is a need, they want to hear every detail. Also, they have an innate ability to feel the pain of others. They are great comforters and loyal to stay close until the circumstance subsides. People with a lot of empathy may tend to focus on the present rather than the future. In general, they can feel the sadness and discomfort that others suffer. Also, they have a strong desire to come alongside anyone in need to comfort them, however possible.

Compassion is like empathy in the sense of being willing to suffer with others. However, for this study it is important to notice compassion moves beyond suffering with others, being aware of their difficulties, and listening to their cries. But for compassionate people it is not enough. Compassionate people must do something; they must act and solve the problem. They tend to think more about the next steps and are anxious to move through the present painful circumstance. They are futuristic in nature. Like people with empathy, they recognize the pain but are quicker to move to a better future.

An example that distinguishes both empathy and compassion can be seen as a nurse takes care of a patient after a particular operation. Immediately after surgery, a nurse may be very empathetic and want to know the pain level of the patient, does the bed need to be raised, does the temperature in the room need to be changed, etc. However, for the good of the patient, the same nurse may come in the next morning and say, "Okay, it is time to get out of the bed and walk." For that nurse, the operation is over, and a new process of action is needed to prepare for the patient's future. The pain of walking after an operation will be short-lived, and healing will be accelerated by moving forward.

Questions:
Do you tend to lean toward empathy or compassion in a situation? Explain.

Do you feel like most people in a small group need empathy or compassion and why?

Give an example when you have felt empathy or compassion from someone in your group or in your church. Was the experience positive or negative?

Contemplate:
Both empathy and compassion are needed in every small group.

Jesus possessed both empathy and compassion

Jesus is empathetic toward all of us. He has heard our every prayer, known our every problem, and watched us in our suffering. In all that, he has shown sincere empathy. But he is also serious about each of us continuing to progress as we fulfill his purpose, whether as individuals or as small groups.

Many small groups are good about recognizing each other's needs, but slow and fearful about encouraging people to step into the future. Christlike empathy is critical for every small group to have. However, without the driving force of compassion, small groups and churches become anemic and spiritually lifeless. Outreach cannot exist on empathy alone. Christian outreach is always fueled by Christian compassion that compels us to solve both individual and group challenges.

Jesus was not only filled with empathy but also filled with compassionate love. Because the world was living in the hopeless darkness of sin, God had seen and heard enough. Something had to be done. The power of sin came into every life, like a tornado ravishing trees and homes, or a hurricane destroying the last harbor for hope. So, in the fullness of time, Jesus came. After arriving and viewing the destructiveness of sin, along with those around him, Jesus declared, *"The thief comes only to steal and kill and destroy; I have come that they may have life and have it to the full"* (John 10:10 NIV).

"The reason the Son of God appeared was to destroy the devil's work" (I John 3:8b NIV). He did not come with the power of empathy alone. Jesus arrived full of compassion to solve the problem of sin. Jesus accomplished this victory by destroying the devil's work on the cross and, in accepting his salvation, we are saved by his grace. Jesus was so filled with compassion he was willing to sacrifice his own life for those he loved. That love led him to the cross. And his coming and dying on the cross was God's greater plan of outreach. God's plan of outreach would never have been fulfilled without the compassionate love of Jesus displayed on the cross.

Now, every Christian is to be involved in God's plan of outreach. Jesus was a key part of God's compassionate outreach and now we are to be as well. Whether clergy or laity, God's will for us is to not only experience Jesus' empathy, but to receive his compassion. Compassion led Him beyond merely focusing on suffering alone. Compassion led him to a cross, and compassion will propel us to carry out his will in ways we never imagined. One of those ways is through outreach, which we will discuss in our next section.

Questions:
Give an example when you felt Jesus enabled you to share his empathy with someone else.

Under what circumstances might you find the Holy Spirit prompting you to be compassionate?

Contemplate:
To be like Jesus we must strive to be more and more empathetic and compassionate.

Our spiritual development will not continue to grow as it should without Godly compassion continuing to develop within us.

What is Outreach?

Outreach is simply an outward action of love that began in the heart of God, expressed in the life of Jesus, and now radiates from our own hearts through various deeds and actions.

Peter and John testified about their need to share their experiences, *"For we cannot help speaking what we have seen and heard"* (Acts 4:20 NIV). Love for God and others is the force behind outreach that compels expression. Such love cannot be self-produced, but it can be received if you ask God to help you love others. Receiving such love is the heart of Christian outreach. God is continually reaching out to prepare people's hearts to receive salvation. Compassionate outreach reveals God's love for humanity. It is a disciple's care for non-believers, both local and global, that places a face and hand to God's grace and love.

In a broader sense, outreach is providing resources and programs that will announce, demonstrate, and attract people to the Gospel of Jesus Christ. This can include activities such as food shelters, clothes closets, Christian counseling centers, and athletic programs such as softball teams. The list is long and ever changing according to the need. These programs or activities are not the goal. The goal is to lead people to know and become more and more like Jesus. We must remember, as important as these ministries are, our calling is to make disciples. That is our ultimate priority.

For the purpose of this study outreach is using these programs just mentioned, and all other activities of the church, is to focus on ways we can carry out Jesus' command to make disciples. Naturally, this includes receiving His saving and sanctifying grace. Furthermore, possessing God's love and expressing it through compassionate outreach is represented well in the Scriptures which we will discuss later. It is through a disciple's prayerful and compassionate action that God is reaching out and preparing hearts to receive salvation. When disciples are in relationship with non-believers, they are obeying Jesus' command to go into all of creation to proclaim the Good News (Mark 16:15).

The word outreach implies we have something to give or provide for others. It also assumes we have specific goals to accomplish and a purpose to be fulfilled. Outreach goals must have more than vague wishes. Each small group and ministry of the church should know their strategy and plan to influence others toward Christ. These goals and plans should be visited and updated as often as necessary.

Some of the goals should be as simple as having fellowship with Godly friends. But there should be other activities deliberately planned to minister to those who have not experienced the compassion God has given us.

Outreach must also be reinforced in our curriculum. Godly compassion must be regularly presented and exercised if it continues to grow. Do not be hesitant to let new Christians know what the purpose is of our groups meeting together. Remind the group that we meet to grow in Christ's love so we can become better disciples and learn how to disciple others. The best way for the saints of the church to grow is to share their faith and disciple others. Therefore, our curriculum should be saturated with this expectation. Whether in a broader sense, a narrow sense, through many activities, or our basic curriculum, outreach is not Christlike outreach unless the ultimate goal is to lead people to an intimate and fruitful relationship with Jesus Christ.

Questions:

How might a person feel differently if they prayed with an individual at the altar at church and the person received Christ, in contrast to praying with an individual on a one-on-one basis outside the church and they received Christ?

How do you think someone feels when they share their faith, and someone receives Christ for the first time?

Is sharing one's faith an option for Christians or an expectation?

Contemplate:

Do not begin sharing the Gospel unless the Holy Spirit prompts you. Do not hesitate to share if He does prompt you.

Everyone may not have a special gift of evangelism in sharing their faith, but everyone has a responsibility to share their faith with those God has placed within their influence.

Why Compassionate Outreach is Important?

In the context of this writing, our purpose and command are articulated in the words of Jesus, *"Therefore, go and make disciples of all nations, baptizing them in the name of the Father and of the Son and of the Holy Spirit, and teaching them to obey everything I have commanded you. And surely, I am with you always, to the very end of the age"* (Matthew 28:19-20 NIV).

These words of Jesus give us clear directions for what we are to do in outreach. They also let us know that making disciples is an expectation for all who choose to follow Christ.

There are several reasons why compassionate outreach is important. Here are a few:

First, Jesus commanded us in Matthew 28:19-20 to share His love, give it away, and make disciples, so others can experience His love. He also entrusted us to teach others what we have learned in our own spiritual journey.

Second, we want every person to have an opportunity to ask questions and share their spiritual experiences with one another.

Third, as we teach newer believers or simply share what we are learning, we are living examples of discipleship. Through sharing others become aware of our human frailties, but more importantly, is our consistent determination to grow spiritually.

A fourth reason outreach is important is that outreach gives us an opportunity to talk to people about living in this life and in the next life. As much as some want to ignore the facts, the Scriptures teach there is a heaven and a hell. Further, there really is a devil who is out to destroy our lives. Some people are fearful to bring up these subjects; however, when the Holy Spirit is leading, we can feel confident in our discussions. Jesus promised us in Matthew 28:20 that he would be with us and therefore we need not be afraid.

The last reason that compassionate outreach is important is that it is a time when we can spiritually love on people by sharing God's story of grace, our humbling experience of forgiveness, our countless blessings we have received, and then let them know, God has no favorites. He will bless their lives as well.

Questions:
What stands out to you the most about the Great Commission in Matthew 28:19-20? Why?

What are some reasons why compassionate outreach is important to you?

Contemplate:
Jesus did not ask us to carry the burden of sin. Only He could do that.

Jesus did ask us to carry the message -- the burden is gone!!

Some Characteristics of Those who Possess Compassion

In this partial summation, here are a few concepts that, when synergized together, propels us forward with Christ's compassion to reach out to others.

We have an empathy to come alongside of others.

We have a willingness to act with His compassion so others can be rescued from a life of sin and participate in a life with Christ.

We have committed ourselves to love God and others, knowing we are to, *"'Love the Lord your God with all your heart and with your soul and with all your strength and with all your mind'; and 'Love your neighbor as yourself'"* (Luke 10:27 NIV).

We have a genuine concern for others.

"So in everything, do to others what you would have them do to you, for this sums up the Law and Prophets" (Matthew 7:12 NIV). I believe the meaning of this verse must include sharing the Gospel because, if we were not a follower of Christ, we would want someone to share the Gospel with us. Simply put, our desire should be to share the Gospel with others just as we would have wanted them to share with us.

We are His proud children and want to let others know what God has and is doing in our lives. Compassionate outreach was impossible when we began, but then we realized, *"it is God who works in you to will and to act according to his good purpose"* (Philippians 2:13 NIV).

Questions:

How does a person follow the Scriptures found in Luke 10:27 NIV and Matthew 7:12 NIV and not participate in the Great Commission found in Matthew 28:19-20 NIV?

Luke 10: 27 NIV -- *"'Love the Lord your God with all your heart and with your soul and with all your strength and with all your mind'; and 'Love your neighbor as yourself.'"*

Matthew 7:12 NIV -- *"So in everything, do to others what you would have them do to you, for this sums up the Law and Prophets."*

Matthew 28:19-20 NIV -- *"Therefore, go and make disciples of all nations, baptizing them in the name of the Father and of the Son and of the Holy Spirit, and teaching them to obey everything I have commanded you. And surely, I am with you always, to the very end of the age."*

If God was going to give us strength to accomplish something in this life, how important would outreach be to Him?

Contemplate:

The greatest power known to humankind is Christlike Compassion!

The greatest miracles of God are found on the street named 'Outreach'!

Lesson 2: Satisfying Our Deepest Need

Scripture: *"I have food to eat that you know nothing about"* (John 4:32 NIV).

"My food," said Jesus, *"is to do the will of him who sent me and to finish his work"* (John 4:34 NIV).

Read John 4:1-26 NIV.

Introduction:

Living a Christian life is more than going through an outward experience, such as joining the church, being baptized, etc. Being a Christian is living life with Jesus. When Jesus approached Jacob's well, his humanness and physical weakness was apparent. He could have eaten sooner if he had chosen to go into town with his followers, but there was something that attracted his attention more than food or his own fatigue and exhaustion.

Weariness can become a major factor in serving God. When we are weary, such exhaustion can cause us to be insensitive to the Spirit's leading and keep us from fulfilling many of our Godly duties. However, when love is involved, such as the love you feel for your sick child in the middle of the night, love overpowers fatigue and all other interests.

When I was a teen, I was asked to speak at a district event concerning witnessing to others in high school. I was at home preparing what I might say when one of my good friends stopped by my house. He had bought his first car and wanted to know if I wanted to take a ride. I knew if I went the ride would not be short, and my being as prepared as I wanted to be for the district event would suffer. I remember standing outside the house with my friend, looking at his car, thinking I deserved a break, but then realized deep within me I had a greater obligation. I told him I could not go with him because I had an obligation to fulfill. That is a simple story from when I was a young teen, but it is a principle I have learned to live by down through the years.

Jesus could have been somewhere else in town with his friends. He deserved a break and was exhausted; however, I believe, the love that compels a mother to get up in the middle of the night with a sick child, or the exciting love to share the Gospel as a teen, can overcome our weaknesses.

In this lesson we will be focusing on the story of Jesus and the Samaritan woman at the well. This story shows how Jesus showed compassionate outreach as he ministered to the woman spiritually and she ministered to Jesus physically. We will walk on three different types of roads, figuratively, and watch Jesus and the Samaritan woman interact with each other.

Let's begin!

The Roads to the Well

In John 4:4-5a (NIV) we read, *"Now he had to go through Samaria. So he came to a town in Samaria called Sychar."* Let me say it again, Jesus was not just tired, but exhausted. When Jesus began to travel through Samaria, he was moving into a hostile zone because the Jews and Samaritans had not been getting along for years. And now, although he felt exhausted, he knew he had to confront the problem. His compassion was stronger than his weariness.

There are times when we are truly sick, and God wants us to pull back and heal. However, if our physical condition would not keep us from doing other things we are compassionate about, our physical condition and weariness should not keep us from fulfilling the will of God. In John 4:4a NIV we read, *"he had to go."* Jesus was being compelled by his compassion.

Jesus loved lost people, people whom he had never met in a physical sense, and he loved the process of telling others about what matters most and watching them respond. Have you ever lifted weights and broken your own record, hit a baseball and watched it soar over a fence, or experienced the thrill of the impossible happening? Jesus not only had a love for unbelievers but, I believe, he also had a love for the thrill of participating in watching someone receive new life.

The Samaritan woman came to Jacob's well at least daily to draw water for her needs. As a Jew, Jesus was not supposed to talk with her because she was a Samaritan. She was very aware of this fact and was also aware Jesus had a need. Sometimes we are so engaged in our own needs that we do not see the needs of Jesus. Think of what she saw: a Jewish man whom she could have ignored, a man who was exhausted, and a man who was hungry and thirsty.

God had brought these two together by way of their needs, just like he does with many of us. Jesus had to go through Samaria because of the compassion the Father had placed within him. This woman had to come to the well at the most unlikely time of the day, twelve noon, because she needed water. The Father had led both Jesus and the woman through the natural "had to's" of life.

Questions:

Have you ever been tired, and someone phoned to talk about a spiritual problem? How did you feel?

Why might some Christians not truly love lost people?

Describe how you feel when you are with lost people.

Contemplate:

When you are doing the work of Christ, there may be times you will be exhausted. Remember that Jesus knows that feeling, and he will give you exactly what you need to carry out his work.

"Jesus…who for the joy set before Him endured the cross" (Hebrews 12:2b NIV).

The hardest thing in soul winning is usually the trip to the well. That is usually when we feel most alone.

The Roads to Understanding

Then it happened! Jesus opens the conversation, *"Will you give me a drink"* (John 4:7b NIV)? When beginning this soul winning moment, Jesus did not begin talking about the weather. He talked about the most obvious, the water and not having a cup to retrieve it. The woman in a proud sarcastic way lets Jesus know he is a Jew, and she is a Samaritan. Her attitude toward him is, why is he asking for a drink from the hands of supposedly the lowest of humanity. Jesus could have walked off at that moment but remained humble. He turned the moment toward spiritual things. He broadened her thinking about earthly water to living water. She did not understand this new truth. She reminded Jesus of his poverty in not having a cup to survive life's needs, as some still see Christians even in our times. Then, because he turned the conversation to the world of religion, she in turn shared her religious knowledge. She was proud of Jacob, his well, and how it had provided for countless people down through the years. Still thriving in pride and sarcasm, she might as well have said it has provided water, at least until today, when a Jew with a great religious pedigree did not even have a cup to survive.

Rather than becoming distracted or being lost in an argument, Jesus returned to the subject of water and emphasized the spiritual. In John 4:13-14a, we read, *"Jesus answered, 'Everyone who drinks of this water will thirst again, but whoever drinks the water I give him will never thirst.'"* The Samaritan woman responded, again thinking only of earthly water, and asked for this new earthly water that would forever satisfy her thirst. Such is the cry of every human as they attempt to make earthly matters satisfy divine thirst. While she still misses the point Jesus is making, Jesus gently leads her closer to a new awareness.

Jesus closed the present conversation and surprises her with a new one. In John 4:17, He asked her to go get her husband and return. She admitted she did not presently have one and Jesus pulled back the curtain of her past. She had been married five times and the man she was presently living with was not her husband. Seemingly speechless and, for the first time, showing her first signs of humility, she recognizes Jesus as a prophet. But trying to avoid the conversation becoming too spiritual, she suddenly shifted and changed the subject.

Have you ever noticed when you are witnessing to someone, they may want to avoid the conversation by talking about what is the best church to attend or who are the real worshipers of God? Jesus did not fall for her avoidance, but simply summarized the whole subject by saying, in John 4:23a NIV, *"the true worshipers will worship the Father in spirit and truth, for they are the kind of worshipers the Father seeks."*

Being overcome in her efforts to debate, the Samaritan woman honestly pulls back the remaining portion of her heart's curtain and discloses her real need. Being at Jacob's well was not enough; walking everyday across the ground that Jacob had given his son Joseph never changed her life of sin. Worshiping in her past religious context proved ineffective and no more than a learning process. She told Jesus, *"I know that Messiah"* (called Christ) *"is coming. When he comes, he will explain everything to us"* (John 4:25 NIV). The questions of her heart were many and, in the end, she was the one helpless, without a cup, until the Messiah would come.

Finally, the discussion could end, and both could go their separate ways. But wait! No, there was no need to wait, because *"Jesus declared, 'I who speak to you am he'* (John 4:26 NIV)." Jesus told his disciples not to tell anyone about his messiahship, but that was in another setting, and this is Samaria. When a woman was thirsty and needed a drink and the religious cups of her day left her helpless, this Messiah declared, *"I who speak to you am he"* (John 4:26 NIV).

Questions:
The religious road of influence the woman referred to included Jacob. What religious influence, if any, have you mostly encountered when sharing Jesus with someone? How did you respond?

What diversionary tactics have people used with you when you shared Jesus with them?

Contemplate:

Jesus answers all the questions we need to have answered. Some questions are left unanswered for the development of our faith, our protection, or the protection of others.

We have talked about the 'roads to the well' and the 'roads to understanding.' Now let's look at the 'roads to others.' That is what compassionate outreach is ultimately all about -- taking the Gospel to others!

The Roads to Others

Jesus comes to all of us today. He comes helpless in one sense, and he comes with a need. He was sincerely concerned about this Samaritan woman, but he was also concerned about the lost people in a place called Sychar. If Jesus had gone into Sychar and talked to people of that town, they probably would not have listened to Him. But if the woman with a poor reputation could be changed and tell her story, they would listen. That town needed to hear from someone they knew. They needed to experience seeing a life that was truly changed.

Don't think for a moment Jesus was using the woman for his own selfish gain. What she longed for had come to pass. From her Samaritan longings Jesus revealed Himself as her Messiah. The days of waiting for all Samaritans everywhere had come to an end. With compelling compassion and outreach, she left her water jar and *"went back to the town and said to the people, 'Come, see a man who told me everything I ever did'"* (John 4:28-29 NIV). Using herself as an example, she asked those who obviously saw the change in her, *"Could this be the Christ"* (John 4:29b NIV)?

This story continues as many people came out from the town and became believers. Jesus was invited to visit the town. He stayed two days, and many more became believers.

The disciples returned with food and urged Jesus to eat. Jesus told them, *"I have food to eat that you know nothing about"* (John 4:32 NIV). Then, referring to spiritual food as His deepest need, Jesus said in John 4:34 NIV, *"My food" said Jesus, "is to do the will of him who sent me and to finish his work."*

The deepest need for any disciple is to do the will of the Father. This is always expressed in some form of compassionate outreach.

The need for compassionate outreach was exhibited by Jesus, the Samaritan woman, the believers in Sychar, and ultimately many others. That compassion made a great impact on the Samaritan landscape. According to tradition, the compassionate outreach of this Samaritan woman continued to grow and spread. Finally, she was brought before the emperor Nero. Because of loyalty to her Messiah and a memory at a well, she refused to forsake what Jesus had given her. Because of her devotion to the One who gave her "living water", she was tortured many times and finally thrown into a well that had no water at all. In the end, her deepest need could only be satisfied by "finishing His work."

Question:

Describe some of the feelings the Samaritan Woman, who had accepted the living water from Jesus and became a soul winner, may have felt in spreading the gospel over the years.

Contemplate:

The Samaritan woman lived life to the fullest, and the life she lived was modeled after a compassionate Messiah. She was willing to both live and die for her God.

God blesses our Godly work with more work for the accumulation of even more spiritual blessings.

In Closing:

Take time to pray and ask God where he needs you to go to spread the Gospel. It may be talking to a friend, sharing a glass of tea, cup of coffee, etc. We, as Christians, have the Living Water available to share so others, too, will never have to thirst again.

Lesson 3:
Sharing the Gospel: Suggestions, Insights, Methods, and Tools

Scripture:

"When he saw the crowds, he had compassion on them, because they were harassed and helpless, like sheep without a shepherd. Then he said to his disciples, 'The harvest is plentiful but the workers are few. Ask the Lord of the harvest, therefore, to send out workers into his harvest field'" (Matthew 9:36-38 NIV).

"Therefore, go and make disciples of all nations, baptizing them in the name of the Father and of the Son and of the Holy Spirit, and teaching them to obey everything I have commanded you. And surely, I am with you always, to the very end of the age" (Matthew 28:19-20 NIV).

Introduction:

The following are some suggestions and insights drawn from what this writer has learned over the years when presenting the Gospel. I had the privilege of winning a stranger to Christ when I was between the sixth and seventh grades. I started my first small group shortly afterward. Winning someone to Christ was a joy and thrill I have never forgotten and has led me to a lifetime of winning others, discipling groups, and mentoring various individuals.

This lesson will give suggestions, insights, methods, and tools to those who are wanting to share their faith for the first time, as well as those who have already found the joy and reaped the blessings.

It is my hope that as you read this lesson many of your fears will vanish, and soon you will reap the harvest of sharing your faith with others.

Let's Get Started on this Exciting Journey

You may think, when it comes to witnessing or sharing the gospel with others, that pastors or evangelists are the ones to win others to the Lord. If that were true, then why did our Lord tell us to *"go and make disciples of all nations"* in Matthew 28:19 NIV? Sharing the gospel is for all Christians! It's an exciting journey to take!

For some, when you mention witnessing or sharing the gospel with others, they may jump up and down with an attitude of *"hey, I've got this. I know how to talk with people, and I can talk them into anything."* That IS NOT what sharing the gospel is all about. It is about being sensitive to and following the leading of the Holy Spirit.

Rather than thinking you are there to wrestle the person into talking about the Gospel, think of yourself as being a guide to what the Spirit has already started.

You are not there to win an argument or sell anything. If you come to the end of a presentation to win the person to Christ and they say no, you are not a failure. Your job is not to win the person to Christ, but to present the Gospel. It is the job of the Holy Spirit to encourage them to surrender their life and become a follower of Christ, not yours.

Some results of not sharing the Gospel with others

We leave other people's salvation up to chance.

We negate everything the Scriptures share about our having a personal influence. To assume we have nothing to do with the salvation of others is a total misrepresentation of the Scriptures.

We are not partnering with the work of Jesus.

We are not sharing ways people can be better citizens, parents, friends, church members, etc.

We personally miss out on being more like Jesus and developing in his image.
We hinder others from receiving divine love.

We miss out on watching others benefit from our spiritual lives.

We miss seeing the creation of divine miracles within a human context that naturally develops our own faith.

Questions:

Of the eight results just listed, what are the top three that stand out to you the most. Why?

If neglected, which of the eight should be considered a sin if not taken seriously? Why?

Exercise:

Have a couple of minutes of silent prayer and ask God to help you with one or more of these eight results.

Contemplate:

Someone influenced someone, and that someone influenced someone to influence me. What steps will I take to influence the next person for Christ?

How and where do you find people to whom you can share the Gospel

Pray and ask God to bring new people into your life.

Pray and ask God to reveal people He has already provided for you – relatives, a friend, a coworker, etc.

Pray and ask God who you have an influence with within your circle of friends.

Pray and ask God to open your eyes to recognize people who are experiencing suffering due to sin's entanglements.

Pray and ask God to give you discernment as to which people under your influence currently need your energies the most.

Pray and ask God to give you wisdom as to when and how you should release new converts to spiritually navigate on their own so you can focus on other people.

Questions:

Some people estimate, we all have eight to fifteen people under our influence at any one time, besides our immediate family. Who might those eight to fifteen people be in your life? Take time to write the names down.

How often do you pray for God to send you to someone who is hungry for the Gospel?

Do you expect people to walk up to you and initiate a spiritual conversation, or do you usually initiate a spiritual conversation yourself? If both, why?

Contemplate:

We are not always to wait for someone else to initiate a spiritual conversation. Sometimes the Holy Spirit wants us to initiate conversations as well.

All Christians should be ready and spiritually prepared to lead someone else to Christ.

Some fears or obstacles in sharing the Gospel

To the degree you can talk to others about your favorite sports team, your children, your grandchildren, your accomplishment of losing weight, your goal to build your own business, etc., to that degree you ought to be bold, rather than timid, in sharing the Gospel.

Some may say the reason they cannot talk about religion is that the subject is threatening to others. That is partially a true statement; however, remember you are under the leadership of the Holy Spirit. If the Spirit leads you to someone, the Spirit has led that someone to you.

You are not there to sell a product; you are there to offer help. People in need of something are usually open to considering a solution for their problem. When you begin, you will not necessarily know the need, but the Spirit will tell you what you need to know.

Pride can be a real challenge for some people and can prohibit them from not sharing the Gospel. They can be afraid of rejection if the person does not repent of their sins. *Once again remember, they are not saying no to you but to God.* Your job is just to go and tell, not go and sell.

Questions:

What is or has been one of your greatest fears in sharing the Gospel? If you are comfortable, please share this with the group.

What did you do to help overcome any fears in witnessing that may be of help to others?

Contemplate:

One of the best ways in learning to share the gospel is to practice doing it with someone you are close to. For years, I have done this with people in different churches. It can be fun if you want to give it a try.

The story of the Samaritan Woman is one of the great compassionate outreach examples in the Bible.

There can be at least five places where someone may experience unnecessary fear when presenting the Gospel

---

1.   Transitioning the conversation to begin discussing spiritual things.

2.   Giving your testimony or presenting the Gospel.
      Note: Always get permission before you begin. If you are using a pamphlet or tract, simply ask them if they would mind reading a short Bible study with you.

3.   Arriving at the prayer time and asking the person would they like to confess their sins?
      Note: Do not be shifting your body or doing anything to disturb the atmosphere the Holy Spirit has created. Once again, move forward with the question, *"is there any reason why you would not want to pray a prayer of confession?"* Continue to be still and wait for an answer. The person is facing the presence of the Holy Spirit and answering to Him. If the person says 'yes', ask them to pray a written prayer you have provided or repeat a prayer you will pray. If they say 'no', ask them one time if they have any questions. If not, sincerely thank them for their time and immediately change the subject. Always leave in a positive manner.

4.   Knowing what to do after a person prays and receives forgiveness of their sins?
      Note: If you feel the person was truly sincere in their prayer then, after the prayer, congratulate them for becoming a Christian. Remind them of what they have

done by sharing a verse such as, *"If we confess our sins, he is faithful and just and will forgive us our sins and purify us from all unrighteousness"* (I John 1: 9 NIV).

Then pray another prayer thanking God for what the individual has done and the fact they have received Jesus in their heart. This prayer should show your belief in their sincere prayer and your happiness to welcome them into this life more abundant.

5. Knowing what guidance to give concerning the next spiritual steps.
   a. Set a time to meet with the individual in a couple of days to get an update on how they are progressing.
   b. If you used a salvation tract or a small pamphlet from The Foundry Publishing or another source, leave it with them so they can review the commitment they made.
   c. Get them started with Charles "Chic" Shaver's *Basic Bible Studies for New and Growing Christians* which can be purchased at The Foundry Publishing (https://www.thefoundrypublishing.com).
   d. Explain the importance of being part of a Christian community and get them involved in a small group in which you are participating.
   e. Explain to them the importance of attending a local church and sit with them at least the first Sunday.

If you are still fearful of trying, just remember, if Jesus, who forgave your sins, transformed your life, loved you through bad attitudes, and provided you control over various habits, can change you, don't you think he can do the same for others?

Furthermore, if Jesus could send someone to you, to say the right thing, to express Christian love in the right way, don't you think he will give you wisdom, knowledge, love, and grace, as you present his message to someone else? All Christians are not to just receive the Gospel message, we are to share the Gospel message with others.

You may forget what to say, tremble, or even faint. It really will be okay. When you recover, just explain you are trying to obey God and ask for their patience. Most will feel sorry for you and let you continue, if for no other reason, to see what will happen next. Years ago, this happened to someone I know. Okay, it was me. The individual not only saw my mistakes, but they also felt my conviction and accepted Christ as their Savior.

In every circumstance remember, when you are attempting to follow God's will, "nothing can go wrong."

Questions:

Of the five places mentioned above where some people may experience unnecessary fear, which ones have been the most challenging to you?

What feelings and emotions have you experienced when you became aware you should share your faith?

Contemplate:
"Oh God, help me to realize someone needs to hear what I need to share."

Because sharing the Gospel is so important to God, he always goes before us and is always with us.

When someone questions their salvation

For a person to relate their spiritual history such as baptism, asking forgiveness as a kid, etc., is not as important at this moment as evaluating how the person presently feels about their present relationship with Christ.

If they are uncertain about presently being a Christian, you may want to ask them if they would like to pray and recommit their life to Christ. A lot of things may have taken place over the years and they may need to renew their present relationship with Christ so they can feel confident going forward.

If they feel the need to vent about their past experiences with denominations or churches, remember, you are not there to pass judgement on the past. When they are finished with their sharing, let them know you are only there to assist in a new spiritual beginning as the Spirit leads.

If they ask you something about the Bible, their denomination, or other world religions, and you don't know the answer, just simply tell them you don't know. If their question is so vital they cannot move forward spiritually without an answer, write down the question and tell them you will try to ask someone else and get back with them.

Contemplate:
God is the only one who can unravel the complexity of people's spiritual backgrounds. Unless He directly gives you something to say about the past, focus on the present and future.

Methods in sharing the Gospel

Methods

Pamphlets or Tracts

This method is usually introduced to the person receiving the presentation by the question, "would you mind if we use this small tract as a Bible study?" Always get permission from the person to share your spiritual faith or to have a Bible study before you begin. For those I have been acquainted with for a while, I cannot ever think of anyone saying "no" to my sharing because I had already laid the groundwork of trust before the moment I asked to make a presentation.

Some see using pamphlets or tracts as an advantage because the presenter basically reads or refers to the material and does not have to rely on memory. Let me just say, it can also be easier on the person being presented to, because they can look at the pamphlet or tract they are holding and can choose how much eye contact they will make with the presenter.

For example, if you are sitting and reading a pamphlet or tract and the other person is doing the same, both people do not have to constantly share eye contact. This can be good because it provides privacy to the person being presented to as the Holy Spirit works. While the presentation is continuing, the Holy Spirit can remind someone of sins that need to be forgiven, give awareness they are estranged from God, and encourage hope within them that their life can be different.

Using a pamphlet or tract can also be helpful when presenting the Gospel to a family member or a close friend because, once again, the focus is on the paper you are holding and, if there is personal shame, it can be dealt with more privately.

To order a salvation pamphlet or tract, contact The Foundry Publishing (https://www.thefoundrypubishing.com).

Conversational Method

As you are sharing your story of salvation or sharing the Gospel in a conversational style, you may want to take a walk, ride in a car, or even sit side-by-side instead of face-to-face, so the person you are talking with will not feel pressure from eye contact. Walking is better than riding because, when the person is invited to pray, it is easier to stop without disturbing the sacred moment.

Your testimony of how Christ changed your life is important and can be very encouraging for someone seeking a better life. But remember, after your story and after the person accepts Christ, they will need more than your story to grow spiritually. They will need someone to share various Scriptures with them to help them become spiritually established and begin to spiritually grow.

Tools for the journey of sharing the Gospel

1. Expect the unusual as God is working.

2. Don't be surprised if God asks you to do something you have never done.

3. Like levels of discussion questions, there are levels of conversations. When you engage in a conversation, begin where the person is, not where you want them to be.

4. Most people have to overcome some sense of fear or unworthiness to present the Gospel. There is always a reason Satan will bring up to hinder your obedience. He may whisper, "that is not you", "you cannot do that".

5. Don't worry what others will think if you go to share your life's story. If you feel the Spirit wants you to share your story, your story is needed by that person.

6. People may experience fear when you invite them to church.

7. When you present the Gospel and someone does not respond with a 'yes' to follow Christ, don't give up. Be open to God leading. Others will respond with a 'yes'.

8. Having a desire to share the Gospel is a gift from God. If you have any fear, think of how Satan fears you sharing the Gospel with others!

9. Relax and realize, the Holy Spirit is with you. I have been in some strange circumstances and can affirm that, *"And we know that in all things God works for the good of those who love him, who have been called according to his purpose"* (Romans 8:28 NIV).

10. Remember that you are called to make disciples. Disciple making means that all Christians are to present the Gospel in some form to all those they have an influence with, or to whom the Holy Spirit leads them to.

11. Never present the Gospel without the prompting of the Holy Spirit. Always be sensitive to His prompting. It may happen when you are in a restaurant, at the airport, or on a vacation.

12. You are not pushing yourself on to people when you are being led by the Spirit. You are simply showing up to help the person to the degree they request it. You may be the one to only sow a seed. Others will come later and water that seed. Remember, it is God's responsibility to produce a harvest.

13.   If you are questioning whether you should share the Gospel with someone and, while walking away you feel troubled in your heart, you probably should return and obey. If you can walk away in peace then do so, knowing God has someone else waiting for you to share.

Questions:

Of the two methods of sharing the Gospel (tools and conversational) which do you prefer and why?

What other method of evangelism presentation would you prefer?

Would you be willing to share with the group an unusual experience you have had in sharing the Gospel?

Would you be willing to share about one of the times someone witnessed to you before you committed your life to Christ?

Contemplate:

"And the peace of God, which transcends all understanding, will guard your hearts and your minds in Christ Jesus" (Philippians 4:7).

Every time you share the Gospel with someone,
you will never be the same!
Your life will be changed forever!
Keep sharing!

Lesson 4:
Sharing Experiences with Jesus and Others:
A Celebration Time

Scripture:

"Therefore, go and make disciples of all nations, baptizing them in the name of the Father and of the Son and of the Holy Spirit, and teaching them to obey everything I have commanded you. And surely, I am with you always, to the very end of the age" (Matthew 28:19-20 NIV).

Introduction:

All of us are to experience life with Jesus. As a matter of fact, the Spirit of Jesus lives in all those who are servants of God. We do not share the same level of anointing Jesus possessed; however, just as Jesus had a divine anointing to enable him to do the work of the Father, so we have the Holy Spirit to guide and direct our own lives.

Each time we share the Gospel with someone, the experience is different. However, there can be similarities in how the Spirit leads. There can be similarities in how Jesus was led by his Father long ago and how the Spirit leads us today. As Jesus lived out his life through his humanity, in cooperation with His Father, surely Jesus shared our questions, feelings, and anticipations in reaching out to others.

Jesus was at a well and was participating in a religious conversation with a Samaritan woman. We may never witness at a well, but the Spirit will lead us somewhere to share ways God has changed our lives. Since our goal is to be like Jesus, we will share in some of his experiences, along with the experiences of other Christians as we spread the Gospel. This lesson is an attempt to merge aspects of what Jesus could have experienced in soul-winning with what many of us have encountered in sharing the Gospel. As you read, compare the thoughts with your own soul-winning experiences.

Glimpses of how the Spirit
may work when sharing the Gospel

Everything cannot be done in a group context. Sometimes, God leads us to do something on our own. When the disciples left to find food, Jesus was alone at the well. This same Spirit will lead us to places that are common, such as a well, a street in the town, or a busy shopping area where someone waits for us and we will be all alone. Down through time, those who have shared their faith have sometimes found themselves to be in strange surroundings.

You may be wondering *what to expect* when the Spirit leads you to share the Gospel with someone. Once again, *every person's experience is different.* However, below is a collage and an assortment of happenings that may take place.

For years, the Spirit has been preparing your mind with the knowledge you would need for this special conversation. Remember that the Spirit has provided you with the wisdom to know when prayerful silence is the best response.

The Spirit gives you empathy and compassion for this person, even like a Samaritan woman who had been married five times and was, to some, considered spiritually hopeless.

There is no way you could have planned for this moment, but the Creator of time, and the One who made the sun stand still, has stopped you for this appointment.

The Spirit singles out a particular person for you to connect with. You receive assurance and instantly know this is the person to whom God sent you to meet. The Spirit gives you an awareness of what to say as the person shares their hopes, concerns, and pains.

The Spirit gives you a warm sense of satisfaction, and you feel joy because you are participating in your Heavenly Father's business.

The Spirit begins to fill you with faith, courage, and anticipation. You know that this person can be changed by God's saving grace.

The Spirit announces His presence to both of you by words and thoughts never planned. Words are spoken freely and there is a bonding like you've known one another for years.

The gift of salvation simplifies life's complexities and provides clear solutions. Life can be different, and changes are already taking place.

Just like the Samaritan woman, this redeemed one responds with the joy of freedom from bondage and hope for the future. A holy countenance testify that God has truly come.

You rejoice that the Spirit carried you, using you to bring new life to a new friend.

You leave recognizing why you were brought to this earth. The former stranger leaves knowing they are in a personal relationship with the loving God of the universe.

**Winning someone to Christ one-on-one is personally exhilarating.
If it had happened in a group, it would not have been the same.**

It is simply incredible what can happen by a well, down any street, and anywhere people gather.

Therefore, when the crowd around you disappears for some other need, don't think of yourself as being all alone. The Spirit is present, and someone may be on their way.

That someone may not know you now, but they will be drawn by your Christlike compassion, and they will be encouraged because you reached out. You, through the Spirit, will give them something they desperately need.

*This is our spiritual payday; this is our victory song!
It is not just that He changes others; our life is changed as well!*

Their new blessing is our new blessing. Their new hope is more than an empty mirage.

Their new life is exactly what we had hoped for, born again, now a Child of God.

Sharing the Gospel Together as the Body of Christ

The next time -- we are not sure.

Who it will be -- only God knows!

The place -- He is arranging right now!

The life -- He has already died for!

The coming joy -- only angels can put into song!

In closing this series on Compassionate Outreach, take some time with your class or small group to celebrate the privilege we have to sharing the gospel. Celebrate that our fears can vanish, our focus can be clear, and our strength can be tempered by His compassionate love. Celebrate that every person won to Him at every well, street, mall, and all places unknown, will gather again, knowing with certainty, "we will thirst no more".

A suggestion to end this series on Compassionate Outreach:

This lesson is intended to be a celebration of what your group has learned about Compassionate Outreach. After teaching and discussing the lesson, share even further ways you, as a group and as individuals, plan to fulfill the Great Commission. This could also be a time to fellowship with food/snacks after your group discussions.

Notes:

Section 3:

Comprehensive Biblical Learning

Lesson 1

Comprehensive Biblical Learning

Scripture:

"Your word is a lamp to my feet and a light for my path" (Psalm 119:105 NIV).

"All your words are true; all your righteous laws are eternal" (Psalm 119:160 NIV).

Introduction:

What is Comprehensive Biblical Learning?

Comprehensive biblical learning is reading the Bible, immersing yourself in its words to learn about God the Father, His Son, and the Holy Spirit. It is having a genuine desire to learn, a willingness to change, and a determination to follow Christ wherever He leads as you read and absorb the written word of God throughout the pages of the Bible. It is also more than gaining knowledge. It is a journey we take to explore and experience all the mysteries God is willing to unravel and reveal in our lifetime. The Holy Spirit will guide us as we are led through God's prevenient, saving and sanctifying graces.

In our day, the primary way to learn biblically should be through personally reading and studying the Word of God. However, biblical learning should be extended to group Bible studies, sermons, on-line ministries, and a whole array of community worship. The Berean church in Acts 17 did not have personal Bibles as we do; therefore, they gathered daily in the Synagogue to search, debate, and discern the meaning of the Scriptures they had.

During this study on comprehensive biblical learning, we will be covering the following topics:

Lesson 1: We will learn what comprehensive biblical learning is, why biblical knowledge is more than learning general knowledge, why we should desire to read the Bible, why we need to read and study the Bible, and the results of comprehensive biblical learning.

Lesson 2: We will study the seriousness of God when it comes to his Word and the mercy He extends. We will explore the Books of Judges and Amos, along with Psalm 119, and observe God's actions and the responses from his people.

Lesson 3: Moving forward in biblical learning, we will consider ways to become more familiar with the Bible, steppingstones for personal devotions, reasons why people may be hesitant to read the Bible, and how the Holy Spirit can teach us in studying God's Word.

Lesson 4: Communicating from Heaven -- this lesson will consider ways the Spoken Word (God the Father), the Written Word (Bible), and the Living Word (Jesus Christ) have been used to communicate God's message of truth to humankind. It will include the involvement of the Holy Spirit in the ministry of Jesus, as well as Jesus' influence on the ministry of the Holy Spirit. It will also consider Jesus' words in the Sermon on the Mount.

The lessons will close with a reading that can be read in unison entitled *"Honor God's Word."* This has been used prior to conventions, church services, and small groups.

Biblical knowledge is more than human knowledge. It is built on divine truth.

Comprehensive biblical learning is more than just knowledge. Biblical knowledge is built on truth. Sin is based on a form of knowledge. The problem with the knowledge of sin is that it is based on a lie. When humankind cannot explain something or have what it desires, the selfishness of human desires plus human imagination come into play to create a world of fantasy. We need the Word of God to ground and anchor us.

As we seek to find spiritual knowledge, Satan wants us to treat the Bible as nothing more than myths, legends, and folklore. All of mythology is based on such empty imagination and various attempts to understand reality. As scientists have explored the environment of space, they have not found Zeus who was the most popular god in Greek mythology and was considered the God of the sky. Nor have they found any other mythological gods, but they have found beautiful order in the vastness of space that resembles the beautiful order in which our physical bodies and earth were created.

Comprehensive biblical knowledge is not built on false knowledge. It is built on truth rather than a lie, on reality rather than fantasy, and on a real person by the name of Jesus that history proves existed rather than the mere images that were created by man. These images could not speak, had no substantiated miracles, and being created by man who came from dust, would become no more than a dust storm.

God the Father is truth. The Bible is the written Words of truth, and Jesus Christ is the living Word of truth. We do not worship the Bible as though it were a god; we worship the true God that informs us through the Bible and communicates to us through the Holy Spirit. The Father, Son, and Holy Spirit are at work to save us from the lies, fantasies, and false realities of sin and restore us to the image of the true God. At the heart of the message is God's grace, his prevenient, saving, and sanctifying grace. All other proclamations of supposed truth are as old as the lie Satan told Eve in the Garden of Eden, saying if she would eat from the earthly tree of knowledge, she could possess ultimate knowledge. Certainly, that proved to be untrue and not only was it the first lie, but it was also the first myth in a world of false mythology.

Why we should desire to read the Bible

We do not read a love letter because we love to read. We read a love letter because we have an inner thirst and desire to better know the person who wrote the letter. Comprehensive biblical learning desires more than a thirst for the Bible. It demands that we thirst after God. We will not continue to read the Bible any more than any other book if our goal is no higher than learning the geography and history of biblical times. We will not consistently continue in personal Bible study if our goal is to only prepare for a small group Bible study. However, when we desire God and desire to know more about how we can have a relationship with Him, our desire to read will increase. In a good way, reading the Bible can be just as selfish as reading a love letter. We have a curiosity, a desire or thirst that needs to be satisfied. Nothing or no one else can satisfy our need. Being a Christian includes learning about God and wanting to know about him and desiring how to please him.

Once again, the reason we read a love letter is because we have a high interest in the one who wrote the letter. The book of Isaiah relates to this strong desire or thirst to know God when we read, *"Come, all you who are thirsty, come to the waters; and you who have no money, come, buy and eat" (Isaiah 55:1a NIV)!*

We come to the Bible with different levels of desires or thirst for God. Humanly, some of our levels of thirst have to do with our ambition to grow. In and of themselves, there is nothing wrong with such desires and thirsts any more than desiring to be married or have children. However, the thirst Isaiah is writing about has to do with spiritually thirsting for God rather than seeking the relationship for purely personal desires. For example, some people attend church regularly, but their greatest thirsts would be satisfying social needs rather than what God desires. Their prayers and prayer requests are all about self-related needs, they have never acquired a thirst to know God better. The prophet Isaiah invites all of God's people to go deeper in their relationship with God, to thirst for the living God.

Loving someone can be both joyful and painful. There are few things more painful than receiving a love letter and finding out the relationship will not progress into something more. We never have to face such feelings of rejection with God. His love for us is absolute and eternal.

The person who does not desire and thirst for God's Word has yet to fully experience God's love and often has not read his love letter, the Bible, from beginning to end. When you have experienced God's love, and have gained daily wisdom and strength from communicating with him though prayer and bible reading, then the thirst grows almost automatically. There is something about the strength gained by bible reading and prayer that satisfies like nothing else.

Questions:

When reading the Bible, which do you tend to pursue the most – information or inspiration?

When was the first time you felt a personal excitement about reading the Bible? Do you recall where you were?

When was the first time you felt a real urgency to share what you had read in the Bible with a friend? Would you like to share your experience?

Contemplate:

Treasure hunters usually find more when they are purposefully digging rather than just tripping over rocks.

Below are some reasons why it is imperative to be immersed in the Bible:

1. I need to know who the one true God is in comparison to other competing gods.

2. As a person who is a live human being, I need to learn how to live in a relationship with a God who is alive and inserting himself into my life by his prevenient, saving, and sanctifying graces.

3. Because I am tempted by Satan who is alive and also inserting himself into my life, I need to know how to protect myself and guard against the influences that will destroy me.

4. I need to know who I am and what I am made of spiritually, in comparison to God who is holy and righteous.

5.   Because I am a sinner by birth, I do not know or understand how to be righteous by my own knowledge and understanding. I must be changed, taught, and trained. His Word promises to be a lamp and a light, so I do not have to live a life of sin.

6.   Because I am weak and do not have the strength to combat temptation, I need to know how to receive power through the Holy Spirit to combat the evil that will otherwise overcome me.

7.   Because I am hungry for more than what all other competing interests can provide, I need to be filled with the only bread that can satisfy my needs.

8.   I need to experience receiving love from the only source of true love and, in turn, learn how to give love back to God and others. Knowing I am loved will change my life because no one can love me the same way as the God who created me and knows what loving me involves.

9.   Because I am incapable of loving others without an inner motivation that asks what they can do for me in return, I need to read about the ways God loves others. Loving others as God loves is not natural for me without God filling me with his love and giving me examples of that love.

10.   The Bible is not to be worshiped in and of itself, but it contains the message of the one I am to worship. It also instructs me in ways God desires to be worshiped.

11.   Studying God's Word will help me spiritually prosper in ways which will glorify God. Spiritual prosperity is a transformation in unimaginable ways as my own will is replaced by God's will. This changing of the will is brought about by the changing of what I love.

12.   God's Word introduces me to God, reveals his presence as his Word inserts new thoughts, gives me new longings I have never experienced, gives me hope for what would otherwise be impossible, and his daily peaceful assurance that will be mine for every day in this world and the next. I need not fear but can be courageous, knowing the God who has spoken to others is now speaking to me. Just as others became a new creation I, too, will become a new creature in him.

13.   I need to read the Bible because it is more than random thoughts about days gone by. The Bible is as alive as God is alive, and as alive as I am experiencing life. Because God sees me and comes to let me know He is near, I will not hide as Adam and Eve, but will seek him by reading his Word and following his teachings. Yes, the Bible was given to us to be read, and I need to learn by reading God's Word.

Questions:

Who/What are some competing gods around you and why is your God better?

Tell of a time when your God defeated a competing god in your life.

Why do you need to read the Bible?

Contemplate:

When we miss our Bible reading time, surely, God misses his moments.

Reading the Bible was never meant to be wasted time. Whether it is obvious or not, every time we read the Bible is Resurrection time in some way.

When I do not hear God speaking, that is no sign he is not working.

Some results of Comprehensive Biblical Learning

Here are some results that can take place as you experience comprehensive biblical learning. The Holy Spirit will enable us to achieve these results as we follow his lead.

1.   This is a time for God to reveal himself to you.

2.   It is a time for you to recognize who you are as you see your own life mirrored from biblical characters.

3.   It is a time for you to feel hope that comes from God's promises.

4.   It is a time for you to experience conviction and correct any wrongdoing.

5.   It is a time for you to recognize the leading of the Holy Spirit as specific Scriptures speak to your own heart and conscience.

6.   It is a time for you to reflect on your past and expand your imagination concerning God's unrevealed future.

7.   It is a time for you to receive the long-term purposes God has for you, or simply know what to do next.

8.   It is a time to get to know God while you wait patiently for questions to be resolved.

9.   It is a time for you to saturate yourself with God's wisdom that may counter the "wisdom" of culture.

10.   It is a time for you to be guided in ways that will produce a greater happiness in this life.

11.   It is a time to learn to love God, yourself, and your neighbor.

12.   It is a time for you to learn submission to God's wishes.

13.   It is a time to become aware of dangers and warnings that will hinder your relationship with God and effectiveness in witnessing to others.

14.   It is a time to have your inner peace strengthened and to explore Godly experiences you have never had before.

15.   It is a time for anxiousness to vanish.

Questions:
Of the fifteen results listed above, which three have you experienced the most?

Of the fifteen results listed above, which three were the most enjoyable?

Of the fifteen results listed above, which were the most challenging?

Contemplate:
Sometimes the Holy Spirit seemingly has more to say than we can take in.

Does your love for God run deep or is it shallow?
God gave us his divine words
so we can know him on an intimate level.
As his children, let us drink deeply in his words.
They will be water for our lives in our darkest days –
water that will never end!

Lesson 2

God Is Serious about His Word and His Mercy

Scripture:

"...I have set before you life and death, blessings and curses. Now choose life, so that you and your children may live and that you may love the Lord your God, listen to his voice, and hold fast to him. For the Lord is your life" (Deut. 30:19b-20a NIV).

"Now what I am commanding you today is not too difficult for you or beyond your reach" (Deut. 30:11 NIV).

Introduction:

The teaching of God's Word and our awareness of God's mercy is vital to every Christian. As we endeavor to obey his Word and sometimes find ourselves straying from his teaching, God's mercy provides paths to recover our spiritual footing. To disregard both his Word and mercy is to live in a spiritually reckless manner that can bring God's judgment or discipline upon us. Our respecting God's teachings and being mindful of his loving mercy is serious to God, because doing both enables us to walk uprightly and not spiritually stumble.

When God's Word and Mercy Are Not Taken Seriously

The Book of Judges

"In those days Israel had no king; everyone did as he saw fit" (Judges 21:25 NIV).

The Book of Judges gives us an example of the great chaos that can occur to any nation or the lives of individuals who do not give due diligence to the will of God. Sometimes when our personal lives become chaotic, God intervenes with his mercy so we can be guided back to the spiritual stability that we need. When Israel needed spiritual help, God raised up judges to rescue them. These judges did not make judicial decisions as judges do in our time. Neither did they administrate the duties of a king. They arose seemingly out of nowhere and attempted to lead Israel to a safe place.

Once my wife and I were on the outskirts of town and were on our way to a city several states away. Suddenly, a car pulled over in our lane and we were involved in a head-on collision. The emergency crew came and was about to take us to a hospital when I looked up and saw a man who had been in one of my discipleship classes years earlier. He was just passing through and decided to stop along the highway to see if he could help. The doors of the car were open with our computers and luggage in the seats. He offered to take our possessions and return them later. There were no spiritual rebellion issues in the case of our accidental circumstance as there was in the outright rebellion of Israel. However, the similarity lies in the fact God brought along someone in the time of trouble seemingly out of nowhere.

The judges rescued Israel out of the hands of their military enemies that God had allowed to test Israel. In a broad sense, the armies of Canaan had been overcome earlier after entering Canaan, but God deliberately allowed smaller armies in various locations of Canaan to remain. He wanted to test Israel spiritually with the intention that Israel would become spiritually stronger through obedience and trust. However, Israel strayed from the earlier commands God had given them and in so doing angered God.

For just a moment of background, let me say, the Mosaic Covenant summarized in Deuteronomy 28 is at the heart of what God expected of Israel during the time of the Judges. Simply put, if Israel obeyed God's commands, they would be lavishly blessed. If they lived in disobedience and disregarded God's commands, they would experience trouble. Deuteronomy 28:1-68 is a lengthy overview with very descriptive details of God's expectations and promises.

The chapter is worth our reading with such concluding verses concerning disobedience as *"You will live in constant suspense, filled with dread both night and day, never sure of your life"* (Deut. 28:66 NIV).

Encouragement and challenge are given to Israel as they follow God's commands. A portion of these verses are as follows, *"The secret things belong to the Lord our God, but the things revealed belong to us and to our children forever, that we may follow all the words of this law"* (Deut. 29:29 NIV). *"Now what I am commanding you today is not too difficult for you or beyond your reach"* (Deut. 30:11 NIV). *"...I have set before you life and death, blessings and curses. Now choose life, so that you and your children may live and that you may love the Lord your God, listen to his voice, and hold fast to him. For the Lord is your life"* (Deut. 30:19b-20a NIV).

Returning to the period of the Judges, we see the time was between 1200 B.C. to 1020 B.C. The last chapter and the last verse of the book of Judges is very significant as we read, *"In those days Israel had no king; everyone did as he saw fit"* (Judges 21:25 NIV).

When the children of Israel entered the Promised Land, excitement was high. God had miraculously brought them out of Egypt by rolling back the Red Sea, had fed them in the wilderness with a special manna to nourish them, and had sustained them in countless ways for forty years. There was no reason to doubt this same God would bless them as they would follow his will. The future was bright, but the hearts of the Israelites turned cold against their God and his commands. They became lawless, self-serving and began to serve the gods around them.

Because of their rebellion, the God of Israel became angry. When they went out to defeat their enemies, just as He said He would do, the God of Israel did not support their efforts. They were miserably defeated because of living in rebellion against God. Then, because of their misery and needing help, God in his mercy, raised up leaders, judges to save them from their enemies and to instruct them concerning his will. God was willing to come to their rescue. He was willing to be merciful. Nevertheless, in time they stopped listening to the judges, and again did what was right in their own eyes rather than following God.

Throughout the book, this cycle of serving the God of Israel, forsaking God to follow their own pleasures, becoming a slave to others, crying out to God, turning back to God, and God mercifully raising up another judge to lead them, is continuously repeated. Again and again, their lawlessness and unwillingness to follow God's commands continually led them to misery. Living lives of spiritual recklessness concerning God's law and taking advantage of God's goodness ultimately led them to personal and national catastrophe.

A key lesson of the book of Judges is that following one's own self-governing laws rather than God's laws will always end in defeat. Also, to ignore God's acts of mercy to intervene will only darken our hopes and lead to destruction. Turning to God and repenting of our sins is the only way to receive his ongoing mercies in salvation.

Questions:

The big battles in capturing Canaan were over because of God's blessings. God left the smaller armies in various places so the Israelites could be tested and grow in character. Whom or what has God allowed in your life for you to be tested and grow in godly character?

At times, when God was giving disturbing warnings to the Israelites, why do you think they might not have been appreciative of these acts of mercy?

Have you ever felt God gave you a specific warning? How did you respond and what was the outcome?

Contemplate:

To receive mercy can include receiving God's undeserved restraint as well as love.

Not even God likes to feel taken for granted.

Let's Turn Our Attention to the Book of Amos

"The days are coming," declares the Sovereign Lord, "when I will send a famine through the land – not a famine of food or a thirst for water, but a famine of hearing the words of the Lord" (Amos 8:11 NIV). The Book of Judges is not the only example of not taking God's commands seriously as we read the Scriptures.

Our world will long remember the Pandemic of 2020. Amos lived in Eighth Century BC and, where he lived, people remembered and were very aware of a great earthquake that occurred in approximately 760 BC. As a matter of fact, Amos mentions the earthquake in both the first and the last chapter of his book. Such knowledge of an earthquake was not easily forgotten during Amos's time, but the Word of God became less and less important in the minds of the people. Although a form of religion flourished in many places, such sins as greed, taking advantage of the poor, immorality, and idolatry were not considered serious. Worse yet, neglecting the Word of God became normal.

Amos was a farmer and a herdsman. He lived in the countryside and would have looked out of place in any kind of city life. However, in Amos 7:15 (NIV), Amos recalls, *"But the Lord took me from tending the flock and said to me, 'Go, prophesy to my people Israel'."* What courage it must have taken for Amos to follow God to the city of Bethel and begin to prophesy God's truth. In Bethel, messages from priest and prophets, as in many churches today, were expected to emphasize such subjects as kindness, comfort, love, and to disregard God's words of warning and correction. Amos was determined to share God's message regardless of the people's expectations. Bethel was a city where education would have been emphasized. They even had their own school for the prophets. At a surface level, Bethel would have been considered religious with proper worship experiences. The problem was the education skirted the messages of God and the worship was only in form. God was not pleased with His people who no longer considered his will as relevant, nor his commands worthy of serious consideration. Therefore, the Lord said, concerning his people, *"I will spare them no longer"* (Amos 8:2c NIV). Furthermore, since taking God seriously and listening to his Word was not important to His people, God decided He would bring a famine of "hearing" his Word. In Amos 8:11 (NIV) we read, *"The days are coming," declares the Sovereign Lord, "when I will send a famine through the land – not a famine of food or a thirst for water, but a famine of hearing the words of the Lord."* This does not mean the Word of the Lord would not exist; it did mean, when given, God's people would be as though they were deaf and would not hear its meaning.

Certainly, we are living in a day when there are Bibles in our homes and Bible studies in our churches, but unless we seriously respect God's Word by making it a priority and submitting to its teaching, we, too, will become as deaf when it speaks. God is serious about what He has tried to communicate to us and serious about how we respond. Any individual or nation who ignores God's Word will, like Israel, follow a path of self-destruction.

From the Book of Judges and the Book of Amos, we see how God reacted and decided to discipline his people. Because they were not willing to respect his Word on those occasions when they needed it and it was presented, they were as deaf. Reading such stories should not cause us to engage in some works theology, afraid of God's punishment and attempting to satisfy him by our good behavior. However, it does challenge us to always listen and strive to obey God because He knows how to manage our lives. To neglect both the commands to truly hear God's instructions and the disregard of God's mercy when he had the power to destroy them caused God to act to defend his greater purpose. From these two examples we should learn respecting God's Word, as well as his mercy, is important to God.

Let's Pause for a moment --

Question:
Do you think we are at this place in our world today as far as becoming deaf to the Word of God? Explain.

Contemplate:
If we are not engaged in God's Word, what are we teaching our children, the next generation, when it comes to reading and obeying His commands.

Let's continue --

Comprehensive biblical learning is as important for us today as for those in the Old Testament long ago. Without God's Word, in a sense, we create our own Ten Commandments, our own beliefs of right and wrong, and explore ways to follow our feelings that can change as quickly as the shifting sands. We create our own doctrines and expect God to bless our thoughts as though they were his.

We create a God in our own image from our personal desires rather than allowing God to create us in his Image. We ultimately see ourselves as able to reshape God's Written Word, the Bible, as culture moves in other directions, and we begin to explain away the teachings of Jesus, the Living Word of God.

Our mind, will, and emotions are always affected to the degree we abandon God's Word. What begins as spiritually floundering penetrates every part of our lives. We become more susceptible to discouragement and depression. Our fears are increased whether real or unreal. We can feel we are always overwhelmed. Furthermore, there is no inward peace because we have ignored what makes for peace. Even worse, our spiritual blindness increases as new temptations are met with weak wills, and adventurous inclinations determine our actions. Our only answer is to return to God's Word.

Yes, our only answer is to cling to the Word of God once again.

Questions:

What differences have you experienced in your daily lives when you got too busy to read God's Word?

What differences in your actions do you think others notice when you neglect reading?

When you have neglected the Bible, has God ever disciplined you in some way? If so, how?

When you have neglected your Bible, what mercies has God shown?

Contemplate:

Reading the Bible is always worth the time, whether we notice it consciously or subconsciously.

When God's Word and Mercy Are Taken Seriously

Had the people in Israel, during the time of the Judges or those in the land of Israel during the time of Amos, allowed a revival of following God's commands, the true satisfaction in their daily living and the experience of receiving unknown blessings would have been realized. People who ignore God's Word from day-to-day surrender God's potential miracles and blessings and may wonder later what might have been.

However, there are those in Scripture who recognized God's mercy and received God's grace to launch out and learn more of God's new teaching. They accepted God's Word as the ultimate reality of their lives as revealed through God's Spirit, and trusted more in his Word and less in themselves.

In Psalm 119 the Palmist had experienced God's discipline and now longed for a new lifestyle that only God could provide. In returning to God's commandments and will for his life, he was not returning to a set of duties to follow or a lifeless code but a living Word that caught his attention and inspired him to obey. As never before, the Psalmist truly believed this was his only hope for happiness.

Whatever the circumstance of the Psalmist, I believe he knew with all of us, the same God, who sometimes allows us to flounder and fall as we follow our own self-serving path, is the same God who opens new paths of mercy and love. Much emphasis is placed on grace in our day, and that is good, but we must not forget the loving hand of God's mercy. That hand brought us back so that more grace could abound. After experiencing his discipline, we love and appreciate his law as never before. We rejoice in what the Scriptures show us and never want to be spiritually blind again. We long for the Word to speak so we can hear the Voice that matters and receive the ultimate wisdom that can come only from the Holy Spirit. As the Spirit speaks, we know we are not alone in our room or the places we journey. The Spirit is there and proves he is the final Word and the ultimate Wisdom as He speaks through the scriptures and saturates our lives.

I believe the Psalmist experienced this as he wrote, *"Before I was afflicted I went astray, but now I obey your word. You are good, and what you do is good; teach me your decrees"* (Psalm 119:67-68 NIV).

The Psalmist also said, *"It was good for me to be afflicted so that I might learn your decrees. The law from your mouth is more precious to me than thousands of pieces of silver and gold"* (Psalm 119:71-72 NIV).

For the Psalmist, what was silver and gold to him in the past had now been replaced by the Word and the will of God. On occasion, we will all have to take inventory of our own lives and see just how valuable the Word of God is to us as we consider all competing interests. When we do, if the smallest tweaking of our lives is needed, even then we will find as in Hebrews 4:12-13 NIV, *"For the word of God is living and active. Sharper than any double-edged sword, it penetrates even to dividing soul and spirit, joints and marrow; it judges the thoughts and attitudes of the heart. Nothing in all creation is hidden from God's sight. Everything is uncovered and laid bare before the eyes of him to whom we must give account."*

For the Psalmist, God's Word was not just an x-ray machine but a cleansing fountain spewing out God's grace and mercy. He is always faithful in everything He says and does.

Questions:

When you think of your Christian life, besides moments such as receiving Christ as your Savior, what event stands out as to when you received God's mercy?

What have you learned from receiving God's mercy?

What spiritual changes occurred because of receiving God's mercy?

Contemplate:

To ignore God's mercy is to test his patience.

To take God's Word seriously is to receive wisdom. To take God's mercy seriously brings a greater awareness of God's love.

"My son, do not despise the Lord's discipline and do not resent his rebuke, because the Lord disciplines those he loves, as a father the son he delights in. Blessed is the man who finds wisdom, the man who gains understanding."
(Proverbs 3:11-13 NIV)

Lesson 3

Moving Forward in Biblical Learning

Scripture:

"let the wise listen and add to their learning, and let the discerning get guidance" (Proverbs 1:5 NIV).

"Instruct the wise man and he will be wiser still; teach a righteous man and he will add to his learning" (Proverbs 9:9 NIV).

Introduction:

Some people postpone their serious bible reading efforts until there is an emergency. Waiting to pick up and study our Bibles when the house is on fire or tragedy occurs is not a good idea. We would probably be too confused to think as clearly as we would like. True, a verse often comes to our mind during such times. However, the Bible was never meant to be a fire extinguisher. It is like a loaf of bread, better eaten one slice at a time. The best time to begin is today. So, let's begin now to explore ways we can move forward in biblical learning and ways we can become more familiar with the Bible.

Ways to Become More Familiar with the Bible

The following are suggestions that can help Christian believers and even non-believers become more familiar with the Bible. One or more or the following suggestions may be used depending on the individual or a small group.

1.   Read and get an overview of a children's Bible story book.

        One of the most exciting small groups I have watched is when several adults with no church background wanted to learn what the Bible was about. Each of them bought a children's Bible story book (e.g. Eerdmans Publishing Co.) and began meeting weekly. Over a period of months, the adults went through the text, reading every story, and discussing how the many small stories merged to tell the full story of the Bible. I was amazed how willing and excited the adults were to participate in this small group.

2.   Read and get an overview of the Bible from another adult text.

        As an individual or group, purchase a book that gives an overview of the whole Bible and read through the sections getting an idea of the Bible's historical and overall plan to redeem humankind. One suggestion would be *"A Thumbnail Sketch of the Bible Story"* by Dr. James R. Hicks (can be purchased through Amazon).

3.   Study various key characters that are involved in the Bible story.

        These biographies can be found in many Bible character storybooks, can be found online, or can be found in specific passages of Scripture. If you are in a group, while studying the characters, periodically divide the group seeing which team can put the names in order as they appear in the Bible. Some of the characters you may choose to study would be:

Adam and Eve	Joel
Noah	Jonah
Abraham	Amos
Isaac	Hosea
Jacob	Micah
Joseph	Isaiah
Moses	Nahum
Joshua	Zephaniah
Samuel	Jeremiah
Saul	Habakkuk
David	Daniel
Jeroboam	Ezekiel
Rehoboam	Haggai
Elijah	Zechariah
Elisha	Malachi

4.   Study an outline of the historical periods of the Old Testament and the New Testament, filling in Bible characters within the periods they lived. This can be played as a game after studying the lives of various Biblical characters.

5.   Study one book of the Bible at a time. Reading a book repeatedly several times can give a real appreciation of insights that are missed in the first setting. Once I read the book of Matthew twenty-five times and, each time, the Holy Spirit helped me gain insight of the powerful message that the author was sharing.

6.   Study topics where you have a particular need such as "having courage rather than fear" or other personal needs. This type of study should be an exception rather than a regular practice. Using special topics are for special times but are not to take the place of developing a broader knowledge of the Bible.

7.   Use devotional books - but only as a supplement to Bible reading. Devotional books, in and of themselves, do not have the same authority as the Bible, and should not replace your reading of scripture.

8.   Studying the Bible in groups. Remember that group learning should not replace your private study time. Both are beneficial and bring different benefits and insights.

9.   Read the Bible with the sincere purpose to develop spiritually rather than just going through a ritual. This may mean reading a chapter, part of a chapter, or just a few verses depending on the guidance of the Holy Spirit. The Spirit may give you a sense of peace to just stop and ponder on a certain verse instead of continuing to read.

10.   Some people try to read the Bible through in one year. However, if their goal is to read the Bible through in one year and not to grow in their relationship with God, then the goal needs to be changed. Keep the main objective as the main objective. – growing spiritually.

11.   Fast reading is good if you are comprehending and putting into practice what you are reading, but it is better to read slowly, if need be, and retain more of what you read.

12.   It is possible to maintain a consistent devotional time in a busy world of parenting, church obligations, working, etc. Stay in a routine as much as possible. For parents with small children, reading the Bible may have to be for only five minutes at a time, or sitting in a car while waiting for children's activities to be concluded. In all circumstances, strive for quality time with God rather than quantity time.

13.   While reading the Scripture in a private devotion, if you do not understand a certain verse or passage, move on to the next verse or passage.

14.   If you feel like you do not retain as much information as you would like in reading the Bible, remember your subconscious is also being affected by your reading. There have been times I have been in a situation years later and a verse would come to my mind that I had previously not remembered studying.

15.   Before you begin reading your Bible, always pray and ask God to bless your reading in whatever way He sees best.

Questions:

How did you become familiar with the Bible?

When you look back at your introduction to the Bible, what would have helped you more?

Contemplate:

As a Christian, everyone must choose specific ways to become familiar with God's Word. Not to choose is to choose not to grow spiritually.

Steppingstones for Personal Devotions

It is imperative for every person to have an ongoing conversation with God. This needs to take place not only through prayer but also through regular devotions. Here are some stepping-stones to consider as one goes through his/her devotional time.

1. **Pray** for God's Holy Spirit to **reveal Himself** as you read the Scriptures.

2. **Read** God's Word **regularly**.

    It is important to form and maintain a habit of reading the Bible. Reading the Bible should not be an afterthought but rather a priority. It is important to realize that just as quality food is necessary for our physical bodies, so good spiritual food is necessary to be a healthy Christian. When occasions occur that prohibit you from your normal daily amount of Bible reading, try to read a lesser amount while focusing on your specific need for biblical intake.

3. **Prepare** your mind as though you are going **to share with others** what you are learning.

    This will clarify your thinking for your own personal application, as well as clarify your explanation to others what you have learned.

4. **Exercise** God's Word **intentionally**.

    This will include ministering to others, witnessing, teaching a small group, or doing other things that show you are not ashamed of how the Word is changing your life. Note: Reading your Bible should not be limited to preparing sermons or small group lessons. You must read to develop your own spiritual life as well as the spiritual life of others. Pray that you and not just others will have courage and a willingness to grow spiritually.

5. **Recognize** spiritual **changes** in your own life.
    Reading the Bible is not a time to be in a hurry, but rather a time for reflection and meditation as one is sensitive to their personal spiritual development. While doing this, there will be times when growing spiritually will be more obvious than others.

6. **Long for** more **knowledge** to serve God.
    As one reads the Bible more and gains more knowledge about the Bible, God will be increasing the desire to do even more things that pleases Him (Philippians 2:13). Do not be concerned about what others may think, such as you becoming too radical about Jesus. Your development may be challenging them, and they are afraid to trust God the way you are trusting him.

7. **Grow** closer in **your relationship** to God.
    Remember that you are not reading a textbook, you are reading God's love letter to you expressed through the lives of others. This love letter will help you grow from your past and secure a better future.

Questions:
Which of the steppingstones would you want to give more attention?

Which of the steppingstones do you feel most people neglect? Why?

For a child or younger person having a devotion, which steppingstones would you encourage the most?

Contemplate:
Walking on a variety of steppingstones can be entertaining, but choosing the right ones is imperative if one reaches his/her destination.

Some Reasons Why People May Be Hesitant to Read the Bible

1.   It can seem to be too complicated.

2.   They may be unsure where to start.

3.   They may be seeking only a quick fix for their spiritual needs rather than getting involved in a relationship with God.

4.   They are angry or disappointed with God because of unanswered prayers in the past.

5.   They may only be concerned about themselves and not about what God wants or needs.

6.   They don't believe God loves them or has a plan for their lives.

7.   They don't believe they can trust God.

8.   They only want to act by the assurance of sight and material evidence, rather than by faith.

9.   They want to serve God only in a group context or along with others. They must realize, ultimately every person is responsible to God, first as individuals, and secondly to a group or church.

10.   Temporarily, people may not have received enough prevenient grace and revelation from God to see that reading the Bible is necessary to mature in their faith development. They may not yet realize that *"Consequently, faith comes from hearing the message, and the message is heard through the word of Christ"* (Romans 10:17 NIV).

Questions:

Of those you are trying to influence for Jesus outside your own family, which one of the reasons might be theirs?

Of those you are trying to influence outside your family circle, which one of the reasons might be theirs?

Which of the reasons, and there may be more than one, do you struggle with the most?

Contemplate:

Reading the Bible becomes a higher priority when we believe it is worth our while.

An Example of How the Spirit Can Teach Us in Studying God's Word

It is vital for a follower of Christ to have a consistent habit of studying the Bible. Our preparation is not only important for us as individuals but for those we influence. Psalm 78:4b NIV reads, *"we will tell the next generation…"*. Psalm 78:5b-6 NIV follows up and says, *"which he commanded our forefathers to teach their children, so the next generation would know them, even the children yet to be born, and they in turn would tell their children."*

This entire Psalm tells the history of how God dealt with his people from the time of Moses in Egypt until the time of King David. The Psalm is filled with history but also includes three approaches in studying God's Word – past, present, and future.

In Psalm 78:7 (NIV), the Psalmist highlights these three approaches when he says, *"Then they would put their <u>trust in God</u> and would <u>not forget</u> his deeds but would <u>keep his commands</u>."* Concerning the past there are things he does not want us to forget. Concerning the present, he wants us to remember God's commands. Concerning the future, he wants us to trust God.

As you read this chapter, do not overlook God's mercy. In verse thirty-nine, God took into consideration that Israel was mere flesh and mortal. He held back his anger and extended his mercy when they did not deserve it. God has done the same for all of us.

In Psalm 78:1-72 we can use these three approaches (past, present, and future) and ask the Holy Spirit to communicate his thoughts to us. Be aware, Satan will do all he can to hinder us from reading our Bibles. However, the Holy Spirit will overcome Satan's efforts and be our tutor and counselor in every matter.

Take time now to read Psalm 78:1-72. As you read about Israel's history, focus on ways the Spirit may be speaking to you concerning your own past, present, and future. Remember, Psalm 78:7 has already given us a clue for the framework of our thinking. Below are some thoughts that came to my own mind but may be different as the Spirit leads you. Let's begin with the past, present, and future.

Potential Applications from Reading Psalm 78:1-72

Remember concerning the Past

Remember you are not perfect, but also remember, neither was the writer of Psalm 78.
Remember to examine not only the list of sins committed, but God's mercies revealed.
Remember our experience of God's grace is limited by our obedience.
Remember God's punishment is a sign, in the end He always rules.
Remember the countless miracles God provided for his people.
Remember we can be so aggressive to fulfill our desires that we forget God's will for us.
Remember the people were living according to their wants rather than his commands.
Remember teaching God's future to our children is informed in his past actions.

Remember concerning the Present

Remember God did not ask them to focus on their failures, but his present commands.
Remember as in a cloud by day or a pillar of fire by night, guidance was always given.
Remember yesterday's miracles can provide today's motivations.
Remember what we learn today, God will not have to teach us tomorrow.
Remember Israel's habit of bad behavior never evolved into God's approval.
Remember the past spiritual experiences are road signs for today's directions.
Remember our questions don't always have to have answers but rather trust.
Remember Israel's disappointments were commas to pause, but not quit.

The Future

Remember all of Scripture moves toward the future and something new.
Remember we are to repent of our sins and not to repeat them.
Remember divine love is the goal for everyone, but the ways we learn are different.
Remember believing God is simply trusting him.
Remember God does not want to fight us, but rather love on us and through us.
Remember past lessons, we never want to walk into the future without God.
Remember having wrong spiritual motives leads us to serving false gods.
Remember how much courage we have for the future will be rooted in the past.

The Bible provides the wisdom to enable us to take all the necessary steps to be spiritually successful in the future. While the future is unknown, we can be at peace in that we know the one who hold the future in His hands.

Praise be to the Lord God, the God of Israel,

who alone does marvelous deeds.

Praise be to his glorious name forever;

may the whole earth be filled with his glory.

Amen and Amen.

Psalm 72:18-19 NIV

Lesson 4

Communicating from Heaven

Scripture:

"In the past God spoke to our forefathers through the prophets at many times and in various ways, but in these last days He has spoken to us by his Son, whom he had appointed heir of all things, and through whom he made the universe. The Son is the radiance of God's glory and the exact representation of his being, sustaining all things by his powerful word" (Hebrews 1:1-3a NIV).

"Above all, you must understand that no prophecy of Scripture came about by the prophet's own interpretation. For prophecy never had its origin in the will of man, but men spoke from God as they were carried along by the Holy Spirit" (II Peter 1:20-21 NIV).

Introduction:

I pastored in a university town for thirty-two years. Once when I was beginning a discipleship class, a young doctoral student from Indiana University walked in and asked if he could join the class. I said yes, he sat down, and things went smoothly. Admitting he knew little about Christianity, in the discussion time he asked these questions: What was Jesus' last name? Was he married? Did he have kids? His final question really caught my attention when he asked, how does Christianity's God communicate from Heaven? Hopefully, the answers I gave passed his satisfaction. The next conversation I had with him included some of the following thoughts.

Let me say up front, the complexity and distinctions of the ministry of the Trinity can never be completely understood. However, there are some specific clarifications the Scriptures share with us while still shrouded in mystery.

It is virtually impossible to consider comprehensive biblical learning without considering the way God has communicated to humankind in previous times, during and after the Bible being written. This lesson will:
1) Consider ways God the Father, the Holy Spirit, and Jesus have been used to communicate God's message of truth to humankind.

2) It will include the involvement of the Holy Spirit in the ministry of Jesus, as well as Jesus' influence on the ministry of the Holy Spirit.

3)   It will also consider Jesus' words in the Sermon on the Mount.

4)   Finally, we will share a bonding and instruction tool that has been used at the beginning of discipleship conventions, church services, children's camps, and small groups to introduce new Christians to the Bible's content and reinforce others of its importance. It is a reading entitled *"Honor God's Word"* that is usually read in unison.

This lesson begins with a Scriptural overview of ways members of the Trinity have spoken and still speak to redeem humankind. Let's begin with God the Father.

God's Words: Communicated in Three Ways

God the Father Spoke Directly to Humankind

Some examples of God speaking directly to humankind can be found in the books of Genesis and Exodus. With an emphasis on the Father speaking directly rather than the Holy Spirit, which will be emphasized later, God speaks to Noah in Genesis 6:3 (NIV) -- *"Then the Lord*

said, "My Spirit will not contend with man forever, for he is mortal…". Then God speaks several more times to Noah, the next time instructing him to build an ark in Genesis 6:14 NIV – *"So make yourself an ark of cypress wood; make rooms in it and coat it with pitch inside and out."* Another example in Scripture when God spoke directly to Abraham (then Abram) in Genesis 12:1 NIV – *"The Lord had said to Abram, 'Leave your country, your people and your father's household and go the land I will show you."* Our final example to be considered here is when God spoke to Moses in Exodus 33:11a NIV -- *"The Lord would speak to Moses face to face, as a man speaks with his friend."*

In all three of these examples, we need to realize, before the Scriptures were written, God was speaking directly to various people working toward the redemption of humankind. God not only spoke directly, but He also sent his Holy Spirit to inspire various writers to share his message with others.

God the Holy Spirit Spoke Giving Us the Written Word of God

In the Old Testament, at times, the Holy Spirit would come upon a particular person and empower them for a specific task God needed to be fulfilled. The Holy Spirit's presence was temporary and was withdrawn when the task was completed. The Book of Judges, as referred to earlier in these studies, is an example of this. True prophets were considered different from the general population because of having the Holy Spirit working in their lives.

As to the writing of the Scriptures, the Holy Spirit came upon various writers directly inspiring them what to write. The subjects and content varied, but all the writings were leading toward the ultimate redemption that God would provide through the coming of God's Messiah.

In the following verses, Jesus, Paul, and Peter look backward in Scripture, concerning the fulfillment of Scripture and the working of the Holy Spirit to inspire its writings.

"He said to them, 'This is what I told you while I was still with you: Everything must be fulfilled that is written about me in the Law of Moses, the Prophets and the Psalms.' Then He opened their minds so they could understand the Scriptures" (Luke 24:44-45 NIV).

"All Scripture is God-breathed and is useful for teaching, rebuking, correcting and training in righteousness, so that the man of God may be thoroughly equipped for every good work" (II Timothy 3:16-17 NIV).

"Concerning this salvation, the prophets, who spoke of the grace that was to come to you, searched intently and with the greatest care, trying to find out the time and circumstances to which the Spirit of Christ in them was pointing when He predicted the sufferings of Christ and the glories that would follow. It was revealed to them that they were not serving themselves but you, when they spoke of the things that have now been told you by those who have preached the gospel to you by the Holy Spirit sent from heaven. Even angels long to look into these things" (I Peter 1:10-12 NIV).

"Above all, you must understand that no prophecy of Scripture came about by the prophet's own interpretation. For prophecy never had its origin in the will of man, but men spoke from God as they were carried along by the Holy Spirit" (II Peter 1:20-21 NIV).

God the Son Spoke as the Living Word of God

Jesus is the Living Word of God. He is the way, the truth, and the life. Both his words and actions spoke and modeled holy living. He encapsulated what a perfect Christian was and was a perfect example of Scriptural teachings. There are numerous truths, too many for us to consider here, when we think of Jesus as the Living Word. However, here are a few thoughts and Scriptures to ponder that are descriptive of Jesus as the Living Word of God.

He is the long-awaited Messiah who brought salvation to humankind. Read Isaiah 9:6, Isaiah 53:1-12, Isaiah 7:14, Luke 1:26-28, Matthew 1:16, and Mark 15:2.

He was born without sin and was a spotless lamb for his sacrifice on the cross. Read John 1:29, II Corinthians 5:21, and 1 Peter 1:18-19.

He died on the cross so our sins could be forgiven, and sanctification could be received. Read II Corinthians 5:14,18-19, I Corinthians 1:18, and Galatians 2:20.

He was both human and divine. Read John 1:14, Hebrews 2:17-18, Philippians 2:5-11, and Romans 1:1-4.

He was tempted in all the ways that we are, or at least to the same level of intensity, yet he was without sin. Read Hebrews 2:18, Matthew 4:1-11, and Matthew 6:13.

He is the Living Word of God. Read John 1:1,14, Matthew 7:24, Matthew 3:13-17.

Questions:

With Jesus being so perfect, how would you have felt being his neighbor? Would you be tempted to move to another neighborhood, or would you want to get to know Him as your neighbor?

When the Bible was being written, the Holy Spirit inspired individuals to write specific thoughts that he was giving them. As they obeyed, the Holy Spirit continued and continued to use their time and energies. Have you ever felt God's presence in a special way and knew you needed to do something in ministry, and then it took much longer than you thought it would? What was that process like, and what was the outcome? Would you do it again, and why?

Have you experienced one of those special times when God seemingly spoke to you directly to do something, and you chose not to obey? Would you feel free to share the outcome?

Does it make you uncomfortable to think of Jesus as being tempted? If so, why?

After all the efforts God has made to send a clear message, complete with detailed paperwork, and showing evidence of his fulfilled promises, can you imagine anyone not submitting to his love?

Contemplate:

Our place is not to determine that God must speak to us in a certain way but to be willing to listen to whatever way he chooses to communicate. Some of his options are: speaking through his small voice, speaking through Scripture, an unusual dream, a sermon, our circumstances, etc.

Jesus and the Holy Spirit's Interweaving Ministries

Jesus Ministered through the Empowerment of the Holy Spirit

Jesus had the anointing of the Holy Spirit on him during his ministry. John testified, that at Jesus's baptism, he saw the Holy Spirit come down from heaven as a dove and remain on Jesus (John 1:32-34 NIV). Jesus did not minister alone; the Holy Spirit was with him. The Holy Spirit even worked through Jesus' humanness as Jesus' helper and counselor. Even in his praying, the Holy Spirit, who is referred to as the "counselor" and "helper", was ever present with him. Obviously, Jesus knew that we, too, would need that special anointing in our own service to God.

Therefore, when it was time to return to the Father, Jesus loved us too much to leave us as orphans, not having the Holy Spirit because, without the Holy Spirit, our spiritual potential would forever disintegrate. Therefore, Jesus made a promise to everyone listening including every unborn child who had not yet breathed. The one in Genesis who had stirred the water and given the first breath of life would breathe into us a new hope and a future. While anticipating Pentecost, Jesus concluded his words in John 14:18 NIV, *"I will not leave you as orphans; I will come to you."* After Jesus went back to heaven and the Spirit would descend, like Jesus we, too, would not have to be alone as Christians and rely on our own strength.

The Holy Spirit's Influence on the New Testament and Our Personal Guidance

Concerning the writing and influence on the New Testament, as well as our own personal guidance we would need, Jesus spoke about the empowerment of the Holy Spirit. The Holy Spirit inspired the Old Testament writers of what to say. Now the Holy Spirit would inspire the writers after Jesus returned to heaven in completing the New Testament. Furthermore, after Pentecost, the Holy Spirit would come permanently on all God's people to guide them spiritually.

It is important to note once again the Holy Spirit's message comes from Jesus who received all things from the Father. Simply put, in many ways, Jesus and the Holy Spirit work in concert for our greater good.

Consider these words of Jesus: *"I have much more to say to you, more than you can now bear. But when He, the Spirit of truth, comes, He will guide you into all truth. He will not speak on his own; He will speak only what He hears, and He will tell you what is yet to come. He will bring glory to me by taking from what is mine and making it known to you. All that belongs to the Father is mine. That is why I said the Spirit will take from what is mine and make it known to you"* (John 16:12-15 NIV).

Questions:

If Jesus has more to say to us, but we feel we cannot handle that information in the present, why might that be so?

After the New Testament was written, the Holy Spirit would instruct us on how to live so we could remain in the will of the Father and the Son. Where do you think most Christians get their instructions to live in the will of the Father and Son?

The Holy Spirit Revealing God's Word as We Need the Spirit's Assistance

When we seriously study the Scriptures, the Holy Spirit is present to assist us. After teaching the Parable of the Sower, Jesus said, *"But blessed are your eyes because they see, and your ears because they hear. For I tell you the truth, many prophets and righteous men longed to see what you see but did not see it, and to hear what you hear but did not hear it"* (Matthew 13:16-17 NIV).

When the Holy Spirit opens our eyes to the meaning of a particular Scripture, we are to take up *"...the sword of the Spirit, which is the word of God"* (Ephesians 6:17b NIV) and carry out God's will. The Holy Spirit enables us to both understand and act on what Scripture teaches.

The Holy Spirit Teaches and Reminds Us

The Holy Spirit's teachings must be based on Scripture or the Word of God and cannot be out of harmony with that teaching. As previously shared, the Holy Spirit gives no personal opinions but honors the messages already revealed from the Spoken Word, Written Word, and the Living Word. Jesus said, *"But the Counselor, the Holy Spirit, whom the Father will send in my name, will teach you all things and will remind you of everything I have said to you"* (John 14:26 NIV).

The Holy Spirit not only teaches us all things, concerning what we need to know, but also in John 14:26 He reminds us of what we have forgotten, if we need it.

Just think about this. If the Holy Spirit is willing to teach us as we study God's Word and is willing to remind us of Scriptures we have studied in the past as we need to be reminded, it is certainly important for us to study and absorb as much of the Word of God as possible. Furthermore, we need to realize to the degree we do not study the Word of God, it raises the question, what other means might the Holy Spirit be compelled to use to teach us and draw us to him?

Questions:

What differences have you noticed in ministry when you were aware you were truly under the influence of the Holy Spirit's anointing and when you were not?

Describe some ways or times you have experienced the Holy Spirit teaching you as you study God's Word.

Have you ever been in a situation where you needed God's Word and did not even realize it, then suddenly a verse came to your mind from your past exposure to Scripture?

Contemplate:

Have you ever considered, it has taken the work of God the Father, God the Son, and God the Holy Spirit, just so you could have a good day? *"This is the day the Lord has made; let us rejoice and be glad in it"* (Psalm 118:24 NIV).

Jesus' Words – The Sermon on the Mount

As Jesus closed his Sermon on the Mount, he told a story about a wise man who built his house on a rock, and a foolish man who built his house on sand. When a great storm came the house that was built on the rock stood strong but the house that was built on sand was destroyed. Jesus likened this story to a person who builds his life with the Word of God in contrast to the person who builds his life on other words, philosophies and hopes. Jesus then informs everyone, the Word of God that was communicated down through the eons of time will also survive because it is eternal and not temporary.

Back to that young doctoral student who strayed into our church and into the room where I was beginning a discipleship class. That night one of the Scriptures we were discussing included the story of the man who built his house on a rock and the one who built his house on the sand in Matthew 7:24-29. The young doctoral student had never heard that story before and I am not sure if he had ever opened a Bible. As we discussed the story, he commented that, in the country where he once lived, a typhoon came and his home had been swept away. He then described it as "there was nothing left."

The school semester was ending. We knew in a short time he would be going back to his homeland. As I met with him later, gave him a Bible, and shared basic truths of the Gospel, it was obvious he was searching, hungry, and looking for something more to life than what he had found.

I am not sure what happened in the years ahead following our conversations. I do know, if God the Father would speak to those searching long ago, if the Holy Spirit would inspire writers to write God's Words of survival, and if the Living Word, Jesus, would tell this story so later a young doctoral student would hear this message, surely the writer of Isaiah's words are still true: *"As the heavens are higher than the earth, so are my ways higher than your ways and my thoughts than your thoughts"* (Isaiah 55:9 NIV).

"As the rain and the snow come down from heaven, and do not return to it without watering the earth...so is my word that goes out from my mouth: It will not return to me empty, but will accomplish what I desire and achieve the purpose for which I sent it" (Isaiah 55:10-11 NIV).

Honor God's Word

Today I honor God's Word, the
Bible, remembering the creation,
the fall of humankind, the flood,
and the tower of Babel.

I remember the Patriarch Abraham
and the birth of a nation.

I remember the Exodus, the
entrance into Canaan, the Judges,
and the Kings beginning with Saul,
David, and Solomon.

I remember the Divided Kingdom,
the Babylonian Captivity, the Prophets,
and the Return of a nation called Israel.

I celebrate the coming of the Christ
in the Gospels, the life of God's
Son, His birth, His three years of
ministry, His death, and His
resurrection.

I recognize the infilling of the Holy
Spirit and the birth of the Church
in Acts, the letters of Paul, and the
General Epistles.

I look forward to the return of
Jesus in Revelation and, even now,
recognize Him as the Alpha and
Omega, the King of Kings, and the
Lord of Lords.

Today, I honor God's Word.

Dr. James R. Hicks
© 2014, 2022
Email: bfcn2@me.com

NOTE: The reading above has been used at the beginning of discipleship conventions, church services, children's camps, and small groups to introduce new Christians to the Bible's content and reinforce others of its importance. It is entitled *"Honor God's Word"* and is usually read in unison.

Notes:

Section 4:

Intentional Mentoring and Equipping

Lesson 1

Intentional Mentoring and Equipping

Scripture:

"You became imitators of us and of the Lord; in spite of severe suffering, you welcomed the message with the joy given by the Holy Spirit. And so you became a model to all the believers in Macedonia and Achaia...your faith in God has become known everywhere" (1 Thessalonians 1:6-8 NIV).

"to prepare God's people for works of service, so that the body of Christ may be built up until we all reach unity in the faith and in the knowledge of the Son of God and become mature, attaining to the whole measure of the fullness of Christ" (Ephesians 4:12-13 NIV).

"then make my joy complete by being like-minded, having the same love, being one in spirit and purpose" (Philippians 2:2 NIV).

"You have made known to me the path of life; you will fill me with joy in your presence, with eternal pleasures at your right hand" (Psalm 16:11 NIV)

Introduction:

Our fourth core principle is Intentional Mentoring and Equipping. In this series of lessons, we will cover the following areas:

Lesson 1: We will consider similarities and distinctions between mentoring and coaching and discuss how Jesus intentionally mentored and equipped those around him.

Lesson 2: As Christian mentors and equippers, we will observe how Jesus chose, corrected, and equipped his twelve disciples.

Lesson 3: We will acknowledge the promises for equippers and discover how to receive the promised blessings.

Lesson 4: We will study Elijah's life as the Journey of a Mentor and Equipper. This will include reviewing his strengths and weaknesses and recognizing God's restoring interactions.

It is important to remember that all intentional mentoring and equipping is under the leadership of the Holy Spirit in a context of God's Prevenient, Saving, and Sanctifying Grace.

In the most basic sense, being a mentor is to help the mentee (person being mentored) recognize the working of the Spirit in his/her life and to help the mentee determine the will of God in each circumstance.

Mentoring and Coaching

In recent years there has been some confusion when people use the terms mentoring, equipping, and coaching. To further complicate the matter, some industries and organizations have defined them differently. In a broad sense, there are certainly similarities between these terms, and there is functional overlap. In this lesson, let's first consider some of the similarities and differences between mentoring and coaching. Then we'll compare the distinctions between mentoring and equipping before exploring while the term "intentional" is so important to this topic.

Some Similarities between Mentoring and Coaching

Meeting together:
> Meetings can be structured formally or informally, on a regular basis, or as needed.

Participants:
> Mentoring can be one-on-one or in a small group setting. Both are observed in Jesus' interaction with the disciples.

Purpose:
> There is a purpose in meeting together. That purpose includes recognizable and achievable goals.

Accountability of the mentee:
> There will be moments of accountability on the part of the mentee to assure the mentor that the mentee is still serious about the objective of the meetings.

Accountability of the mentor:
>There is an accountability on the part of the mentor pertaining to the time commitment that will be involved. Also, the mentor is responsible to maintain a sincere interest concerning the relationship and the process of meeting together.

Assessment tests:
>There may be a personality test, a spiritual gift's test, or other assessment tests for both the mentor and mentee to take.

Continuation of meetings:
>Whether a mentor and mentee continue to meet may depend on whether the purpose, goal, or the commitment levels have changed.

Some Distinctions between Mentoring and Coaching

Relationships:
>Mentoring is built on being transparent and comfortable in the presence of each other. This is not as necessary with coaching.

Listening:
>A priority for any mentor is to have strong listening skills. Both mentor and mentee should have a genuine commitment to listen to each other. Coaching usually involves the mentee listening much more as the coach instructs.

Financial cost:
>Usually in mentoring, there is no financial cost involved. Many times, there is a financial cost to the mentee in coaching.

Contracts:
>Mentoring rarely has written contracts, although there are verbal understandings. In coaching, written contracts may be written to define the purpose, goals, cost, expectations of both coach/ mentor and mentee, etc.

Curriculum:
>There may not be any formal curriculum in mentoring. The life and goals of the mentee becomes the developing curriculum. In coaching there is usually a curriculum involved, along with an assessment test, to help the coach determine where to begin and how much progress is being achieved along the way.

Questions:

Why might some people prefer to be coached rather than mentored?

What personal satisfactions would make it worthwhile in being a mentor or coach?

If you were mentoring someone, what might be some expectations you would have for the mentee?

Why might some people need to meet with their mentor or coach on an individual basis and others in a group setting?

Contemplate:

The mentor's assurance: A generation from now people may have never heard my name, but they will know my ways.

I want my words to resonate Scripture so when I am gone the Word will not return void.

Mentoring and Equipping

I Am Still Learning

Some Descriptions of Mentoring

Formal mentoring:
> The mentor is being observed by someone else or by a small group.

> The mentor will listen to the mentee and give guidance as needed.

> The mentor will also observe as particular skills are practiced by the mentee and recommend suggestions as needed.

Informal mentoring:
> When someone is observing the mentor's actions without the mentor knowing it, the mentee will later attempt to parrot what has been observed. This is a well-known practice in many areas, whether athletics, music, preaching, mentoring, etc. In Scripture, John 19:38-42 NIV, Joseph of Arimathea and Nicodemus fall into this category and are thought of as "secret disciples".

In the early stages of observation, the mentee may not be aware of the increasing desire to be mentored or to be influenced by the mentor.

In later stages, the desire to be mentored increases and the awareness of the need becomes more pronounced in the life of the mentee.

The goal of Christian mentoring is to become more like Christ. Paul understood the joy of mentoring others when he wrote, *"We loved you so much that we were delighted to share with you not only the gospel of God but our lives as well, because you had become so dear to us"* (1 Thessalonians 2:8 NIV).

Mentoring is actively desiring and practicing to bring about change.

Some descriptions of equipping

Equipping is being prepared through formal training such as seminars and workshops.

Equipping for a given task can take place through both awareness and an unawareness of future needs.

Equipping is the activity of being given tools, such as books, so training can take place. Equipping may also take place through those who share a vision of what is possible. As with all equipping, this, too, can be part of the Holy Spirit's work through Prevenient, Saving, and Sanctifying Grace.

Equipping, in a Christian sense, is learning what it means to be Christlike primarily through knowledge and understanding. Paul wrote, *"May the God of peace,...equip you with everything good for doing his will, and may he work in us what is pleasing to him, through Jesus Christ, to whom be glory forever and ever. Amen"* (Hebrews 13:20a-21 NIV).

Equipping is actively learning and planning to bring about change.

Questions:

Did the people who mentored you the most do so through formal or informal mentoring?

Do you prefer to learn through formal or informal mentoring, and why?

If you were mentoring someone, what negative habit or characteristic in the life of the mentee might frustrate you the most?

Contemplate:

Sometimes when God wants us to accomplish something great and we do not have the skills, He can send us a mentee who has different skills to assist us.

To accomplish great things, sometimes you need to choose mentees who can do things you cannot. Just help them to catch the vision of what God might do through them, and allow God to fulfill that vision.

The Intentional Life

Underneath all our attempts to mentor or equip anyone spiritually, we must have a genuine desire to help them find and to do God's will. Our intention is to be in alignment with God's wisdom as communicated through his Spirit. God provides the spiritual direction for us to follow.

God sent his Son with an intention to redeem sinful humanity. Jesus came with an intention to obey the Father's will and bring abundant life to those who follow him (John 10:10). The Holy Spirit was sent intentionally to take Jesus' place and fulfill such actions as convicting us of our sins, empowering us, etc. We intentionally raise our children in certain ways. We intentionally choose the church we attend. We intentionally set goals and even solve problems from a framework of our intentions.

Deciding on our intentions is important because it shapes our priorities and our identity. If we want to know what a person may do in the future, sometimes we only need to look at the person's past record of the actions he/she chose to do and what was left undone. That person's intentions at that time will be revealed.

The Psalmist had settled the question about his present and future when he declared, *"in God I trust; I will not be afraid. What can man do to me? I am under vows to you, O God; I will present my thank offerings to you. For you have delivered me from death and my feet from stumbling, that I may walk before God in the light of life"* (Psalm 56:11-13 NIV).

To act intentionally in a spiritual sense is to be deliberate in our actions.

Questions:

What do you think might be one of the biggest struggles for Christians in your age group that hinders them in being spiritually intentional?

Why might people be more intentional about their children's public education than their children's Christian education in a church setting?

Contemplate:

Sometimes people understand our intentions before we do.

One Reason Jesus Became More Intentional

Jesus' method of discipleship was intentional mentoring and equipping. Jesus used both as he worked with individuals and small groups, chiefly his twelve disciples. However, before he selected the twelve, there was an event that, I believe, strengthened his resolve to be intentional.

In Mark 3:1-6 NIV, we find the story of the man with the shriveled hand. Jesus went into the synagogue and found him there. This was taking place on the Sabbath and, possibly, the Pharisees had placed the man there to trap Jesus. They watched closely to see if Jesus would violate "their" law and heal the man on the Sabbath.

Jesus brought the man up front and placed him in the middle of the Pharisees so everyone could see him. He then asked them questions intending to draw out their feelings of compassion for the man. Their silence revealed their hard hearts and he became angry. The observance of the law was more important to them than the suffering of the man and the need for healing.

The anger Jesus felt toward the Pharisees was momentary. The anger reflected the grief that surged through Jesus' heart. He was sympathetic towards the man's need, but those representing the religious community of the day seemingly had no sympathy. The Pharisees could not see that the shriveled hand of the man also represented how, over time, their own hearts had become spiritually numb and spiritually lifeless for the work of God.

Jesus asked the man to stretch out his hand and his hand was completely restored. Obviously, the man was overjoyed. However, the Pharisees were frustrated. Jesus had overcome their trap and challenged their understanding of God's will as expressed through the Law.

The Pharisees didn't come to their misunderstanding of the Law quickly. They were well schooled in understanding each word, each sentence. I can imagine them setting down and enjoying long conversations about various aspects of the law. In a number of ways their interpretation of the Law had become their god, their identity. And they felt they need to protect that identity to the death. There was too little room in their thought processes for new understandings or even mercy toward a man with a shriveled hand. There was strong resistance to what God might be doing through this Jesus.

If there is one weakness that mentors or coaches have to this day it is the lack of intentionality. Some mentors have become so involved in the work and activity of the church that they have forgotten God's real purpose is for us, making Christlike disciples. Like Jesus, those who mentor

114

and equip others should have a natural emotional response that is repulsed by the sight of what evil can do. The shriveled hand can represent many examples of the ongoing activity of sin that will ultimately destroy what is good within all of us.

Being spiritually intentional is not normal for any of us. It takes continual effort and discipline. We must not only respond in an affirmative way to God's Prevenient, Saving, and Sanctifying Graces, but we must guard and protect God's work as it grows and develops within us. This is done by remaining spiritually intentional.

Good habits, recreational pleasures, and even church activities must never rob us of the energy we will need to remain intentional. As a matter of fact, when the Spirit of God visits our small groups and churches, like the Pharisees, we, too, will miss his presence unless we are spiritually sensitive and intentional in our focus. If you want to see how Jesus is working daily, you must be looking for him.

No doubt, we are all surrounded and will remain surrounded with evil influences until Jesus comes back. However, as mentors and equippers, we do not have to absorb evil's influence and, over time, become spiritually numb. To forget the horrific cost of sin and casually get accustomed to sin's surrounding presence will always leave us with calloused hearts and an insensitivity to God's plan. When that happens, any mentoring or equipping becomes a lifeless routine from which no spiritual purpose will be achieved.

Mentors and equippers are to genuinely strive to be like Jesus. Jesus could not only experience love, but he could also experience anger concerning evil's presence. Whenever Christians get to the place where they are no longer emotionally bothered by the disease of sin, they have lost their desire to be Christlike.

One of Jesus' characteristics that proved he was pure and holy was his repulsion of evil. One of the most holy acts he carried out was becoming angry at the existence of evil. He never lost control in his anger, but he used it as a launching pad to carry out God's next big purpose. He healed the man with the shriveled hand and then would go ordain his apostles to carry out other holy activities in kind.

Questions:

The Pharisees were not going to allow Jesus to minister in a way they were not accustomed to. What is an illustration in your life that revealed you needed to change so Jesus could work in a new way?

If a particular Christian develops a casual attitude toward sin and is no longer emotionally bothered by its existence, does this grieve the Spirit of Jesus, and might such an attitude make him angry?

Do you find it harder to remain spiritually intentional around those who are Christians or those who are not?

Contemplate:

Being intentional is an ongoing activity that progresses and grows as we develop through Prevenient Grace, Saving Grace, and Sanctifying Grace.

The man with the withered hand was a testimony of what the disease of sin can do. Jesus gave a testimony of what he can do to sin.

Heavenly Father,

May I always be intentional in all that I do and speak.
As I follow in Your footsteps, lead me
to those who need to be mentored and equipped.
Give me the strength and wisdom
to know what to do, what to say,
and then be willing to let go.
In your footsteps I found power to be a mentor!

Lesson 2

Jesus' Mentors and Equippers

Scripture:

"You did not choose me, but I chose you and appointed you to go and bear fruit - fruit that will last. Then the Father will give you whatever you ask in my name. This is my command: love each other" (John 15:16-17 NIV).

"One of those days Jesus went out to a mountainside to pray and spent the night praying to God. When morning came, he called his disciples to him and chose twelve of them, whom he also designated apostles: Simon (whom he named Peter), his brother Andrew, James, John, Philip, Bartholomew, Matthew, Thomas, James son of Alphaeus, Simon who was called the Zealot, Judas son of James, and Judas Iscariot, who became a traitor" (Luke 6:12-16 NIV).

Introduction:

No one was to be born and then die without leaving a Christian legacy and a lasting witness. We were born not only to receive Prevenient Grace, Saving Grace, and Sanctifying Grace but also to tell our stories of how and when we experienced these graces. Some may not be ready to hear and understand deeper theological terms, and you may not be able to fully explain those terms yet. But there are some things God has taught you from life's experiences and you do know for certain. As the blind man said, *"...One thing I do know. I was blind but now I see"* (John 9:25b NIV)! One of the greatest tools every disciple has in witnessing for Christ is to tell how God has changed and affected his/her own life. Further, as Jesus works in all our lives, he will bring others around us who will ask questions and open an opportunity for us to tell our stories.

Jesus not only wants us to share our stories but also to come alongside others so they will be mentored and equipped to do God's will. In this session we will cover: Jesus chooses his twelve; Jesus giving moments of correction; and remembering the mentors.

Join me as we see how Jesus chooses his twelve.

117

Jesus Chooses His Twelve

It is a critical time in the life of Jesus. Some of those who followed him from place to place were just curiosity seekers; yet they were considered his disciples. From those disciples and other individuals Jesus met along the way, he would choose twelve special disciples who we think of as his original apostles. In today's world we mix the terms apostles and disciples. In this study, unless distinguished otherwise, we, too, will be referring to the twelve using both terms. The twelve he is about to choose are the ones he will invest his time and energy in for the greatest portion of his earthly ministry with an intention of mentoring and equipping them. These followers are to become his future mentors and equippers of others. Before choosing his disciples, we see in Luke 6:12 (NIV) that Jesus spent an entire night in prayer seeking the will and wisdom of the Father. So, it is for all of us in our ministries as clergy or laity. Every part of our mentoring and equipping must be under divine direction.

It is important to note that Jesus chose his own disciples whom he would mentor. No one chose them for him. We will talk more about this as our series of mentoring and equipping unfolds. For now, let's also realize, Jesus chose the number twelve because it represented the twelve tribes of Israel.

Jesus really knew how to build a team. He established an atmosphere for good communication, a sense of oneness as a group, and a clear purpose of mission. Jesus' team represented a variety of backgrounds including four men who were fishermen, and one who was an educated tax collector. Another would have been considered an activist concerning the politics of his day. The Bible does not tell us the exact ages of his twelve disciples but all of them would have probably been younger than thirty years old. I once heard someone say, Jewish young men could seek out a rabbi for mentoring when they were in their early teen years. Also, they could choose to remain under the tutorage of the rabbi until the age of thirty. If this is true, Jesus was not an exception to this method as he started his public ministry at approximately age thirty and began mentoring others. Two methods of mentoring were normally used at that time: one-on-one mentoring, and group mentoring within a context of a small group. Most of Jesus' mentoring was done in this latter context.

The primary purpose for Jesus to have disciples was so they could be mentored and trained by him to go forth and carry out his preaching ministry. Secondly, the disciples were to learn from Jesus lessons for character development as well as equipping them for works of service. It would have been impossible for them to become like their mentor without living life with him. To occasionally be in his presence or occasionally giving him some of their time would never be enough to absorb all he wanted to share. Thirdly, they would need to become witnesses to others concerning Jesus' miracle-working power. To emotionally absorb the feelings of hearing demons scream in fear, or hear the shout of victory when someone was healed, needed a firsthand experience.

By living in his presence, the twelve disciples would truly learn who Jesus is. Jesus may have told parables to the onlookers and curiosity seekers, but these disciples would have private times when Jesus opened his heart about multiple aspects of being a mentor, an equipper, and a true disciple. Living alongside Jesus, they would not only watch him perform public miracles, but they would also watch him in private, personal moments. For those he would simply trust God to provide in other ways. Further, they would sense Jesus' loneliness while watching him reach out for their friendships and watch him accept their friendships while growing in trust and vulnerability.

Jesus left everything to come, find, and choose his twelve. The disciples left everything to go, find, and choose Jesus' new life. Both Jesus and his twelve found the rewards of a mentor are worth dying for.

Questions:

How might you have felt if you met Jesus and he invited you to be his disciple?

Which one of your friends would you invite to "come and see" Jesus and why?

If the disciples were so diverse in their backgrounds, what might have excited them about coming together?

What might have been a mentoring action that Jesus performed?

What might have been an equipping action Jesus performed?

If you were to spend three years with Jesus, what would you hope to learn, or how would you like to be changed?

Describe as much as possible what you think Jesus' loneliness was like.

Contemplate:

My calling to be a disciple of Jesus is just as valid as any of the original twelve.

Helping to keep their stress level down, the group of disciples must have had a lot of fun times as well as tough times.

Jesus Giving Moments of Correction

Campfire conversations stimulated many new thoughts. Walking down roads and having leisurely chats must have raised many speculations. Conversations were also a reaction to the new encounters of disappointing moments. During such times, Jesus would protect his disciples by correcting them as needed. Like the disciples, when we walk down our roads and can't see where they may be leading, we grasp the hand of Jesus and hold tightly to it. As He protects and corrects us while walking alongside us, we feel the love radiating from him as he mentors us. Even today, mentoring and equipping involves "protecting by correcting" just as it did when Jesus mentored and equipped his disciples.

When the rich young ruler turned and walked away because Jesus was seemingly asking him to sacrifice too much, Peter looked seriously at his own future and the future of the other disciples and said to Jesus, *"...We have left everything to follow you"* (Mark 10:28 NIV)! That was an honest reflection and feeling from Peter's heart. Jesus replies to him by saying, *"I tell you the truth"* (Mark 10:29 NIV). When Jesus responds to anyone by saying, *"I tell you the truth"*, the whole world can feel confident what will be said is the truth. In Mark 10:29-31 (NIV) we read *" 'I tell you the truth,' Jesus replied, 'no one who has left home or brothers or sisters or mother or father or children or fields for me and the gospel will fail to receive a hundred times as much in the present age...and in the age to come, eternal life. But many who are first will be last, and the last first.' "* Jesus obviously appreciated that special moment when Peter was honestly sharing his feelings, but Jesus also felt it necessary to give a gentle correction so Peter's thinking would not lead him toward a feeling of self-pity.

This was not the only time Peter had a weakness in overly comparing himself with others. The fact is all of us can have tendencies that might lead us away from fully trusting Jesus. As great as Peter was, even at the level of being the lead disciple in the group, this tendency repeated itself again just before Jesus was about to ascend back to Heaven.

In John 21:18-22 NIV, Jesus is explaining to Peter the kind of death he will go through to glorify God. Jesus said to Peter once again, *"...Follow me"* (John 21:19b NIV)! Next, we are told that Peter turned and sees that the Apostle John is also following Jesus along with Peter. Then it happened! Peter begins to compare himself with John. *"When Peter saw him, he asked, 'Lord what about him?' Jesus answered, 'If I want him to remain alive until I return, what is that to you? You must follow me' "* (John 21:21-22 NIV).

The truth is Jesus does not have to tell us everything going on in his Kingdom, his church, or even among other disciples that are around us. To live a life of comparisons can lead to jealousy, self-pity, a feeling of worthlessness toward self, and even anger towards God. On the other hand, it can lead to pride, arrogance, and a lack of Christian humility.

Jesus knew Peter had, once again, made an error in judgment. Jesus, once again, gently corrected Peter and, once again, Jesus, the great mentor and equipper, simply told him -- keep on following me.

Questions:

Why might conversations that are concerned with "simply sharing information" lead to personally comparing ourselves with others?

What can be helpful so we do not compare ourselves so much with others?

Do you feel sorry for Peter because Jesus corrected him, and if so, why?

How do you think Jesus felt by having to correct Peter?

When was a time in your life you felt the correction of God? How did the correction make you feel?

If your spiritual leader gently corrected you, how would you feel and why?

Contemplate:

People who never see a need to correct others probably possess few life experiences or a lack of wisdom.

Gentle correction can be a way to say I love you and I also love me.

Remembering the Mentors and Equippers

Thank You

No one will continue in the ministry of mentoring and equipping if they have purely selfish motives. One of the challenges of Jesus was to work with the twelve men who were learning the joy of blessing others and keeping their egos in balance. Dealing with ego needs were an issue as the disciples grew from grace to grace.

Scripture does not share the history of everyone's life equally or give equal exposure to all the labors and efforts that every disciple put forth. Because Scripture gives some disciples more attention than others, some have wondered which of the disciples would have been closer to Jesus.

The truth is, no one really knows, and the fact is, Jesus was probably close to all of them in different ways. However, according to what we know of their personalities, the culture, and how they related to Jesus, they may have displayed their closeness by the way they positioned themselves in seating positions. While Scripture is not explicit in the sitting arrangements, let's set them according to personality needs and levels of connectedness to others.

We see Peter, Andrew, James, and John would be right up next to Jesus, two of them on each side of him. Expanding further around the circle on each side of Jesus might be Philip, Bartholomew (Nathaniel) on one side, and Matthew and Thomas on the other. And extending still further from Jesus going around the circle might be James, son of Alphaeus, Simon who was called the Zealot, Judas (Jude) son of James, and Judas Iscariot, the traitor rounding out the circle.

In addition, it is interesting to notice that after Acts 2, we no longer are told about the lives of five of the disciples in the Scriptures. Tradition tells us where these disciples went, what they accomplished, and how they died, but Scripture is silent on such subjects.

Let me say it again, if we want to continue as mentors and equippers we must have correct motives. We should not mentor and equip because we want our names to be well known like Peter, James, and John. We should not continue mentoring and equipping because we desire a special anointing or miracles. We should continue to follow Jesus in mentoring and equipping because of the inward joy and personal satisfaction of living life with the Master.

After three years with Jesus, it seems to be recognized as one of the original twelve, each follower had to have been an eyewitness to the ongoing ministry of Jesus, have witnessed Jesus going to the cross, and have witnessed seeing him alive afterwards. Like Jesus, the honor of being about the Father's business meant more than personal fame. As a matter of fact, studies have revealed that all twelve of the disciples, excluding John who died of old age, suffered and died a martyr's death. Looking back, for virtually half of the original twelve, no one ever recorded with verifiable evidence how they died, how many watched when they were tortured, or if any of these had a proper burial.

At the core of why the disciples began to follow Jesus was how they felt drawn toward something they had not yet experienced, the coming of the Kingdom. Also, listening to Jesus and watching him meant more to them than everything else. Let us remember that the one who cares for the lilies of the field and watches sparrows fall is also watching over our mentoring and equipping. When we pass from this life and enter the next, we will see our God who *"does not show favoritism"* (Romans 2:11 NIV).

Questions:
Can you share some brief thoughts about a particular Christian who goes out of his/her way to help others and gets little recognition?

Can you explain the difference you feel when you hear a "well done" from the crowd and sensing a "well done" from the Holy Spirit?

Can you share some way you have become like one of your mentors?

Can you share how you feel when you catch yourself acting, behaving, or thinking like your mentor?

Would you say a short prayer and thank Jesus for one special thing you may never have learned without the mentor he sent your way?

Exercise:

If you could write a thank-you note to someone who has mentored you, what would you like to say to him/her?

Contemplate:

Mentoring someone is not just influencing them to do something; it is them learning to be something.

Don't forget to pray for your mentor daily.

Also, send a thank-you note to your mentor expressing your appreciation for all he/she has done for you.

Lesson 3

Promises for Equippers

Scripture:

"Looking at his disciples, he said: "Blessed are you who are poor, for yours is the kingdom of God. Blessed are you who hunger now, for you will be satisfied. Blessed are you who weep now, for you will laugh" (Luke 6:20-21 NIV).

"But I tell you who hear me: Love your enemies, do good to those who hate you, bless those who curse you, pray for those who mistreat you" (Luke 6:27-28 NIV).

"Do to others as you would have them do to you" (Luke 6:31 NIV).

Introduction:

We never know what life will throw our way. One day I was surprised as I met up with this skunk family that was probably no more than ten feet from me. With the little knowledge I knew about skunks, I thought I needed to stand still, not move, and let them quietly move along at their own speed. This made me think how we, as equippers, need to know what to do and what to expect when we are equipping others. This lesson will deal with promises we can be assured of as we look at the blessings Jesus promised his disciples when he shared the Beatitudes with them.

We not only need to experience Christian fellowship and life experiences in a small group, but also need to have specific training for present and future experiences. In the Sermon on the Mount (Matthew, chapters 5-7), Matthew wrote in great length and detail as he listed nine Beatitudes. Because of a different purpose in writing, Luke lists four Beatitudes that give foundations for the equipping or training that will follow. In this lesson we will begin with these four expectations followed by "Where to Begin" and "How to Receive the Blessings".

Training was important to Jesus as he taught his disciples. In Matthew we read, *"...His disciples came to him, and he began to teach them..."* (Matthew 5:1b-2a NIV). Training or equipping was important to Jesus in Luke's gospel as well. All along the way, the disciples had times of lighthearted fun, but there were also times of serious instruction, when Jesus commanded their respect and attention. Luke wants to emphasize the intensity and how intentional Jesus was at this moment when we read the words, *"Looking at the disciples..."* (Luke 6:20a NIV). It was an important moment for this new family of Jesus' followers, and Jesus wanted to explain the expectations for each disciple, as well as what they could expect from him. In Luke 6, Jesus begins more earnestly to prepare these men to be his skilled mentors and equippers who will ultimately change the world through his Spirit. He wants to prepare all of us to do the same.

Now, let's consider what makes up a true disciple in Luke 6 who will mentor and equip others. Let's also be aware of the promises that are provided for each circumstance.

A Promise to the Poor

Even Jesus, the Son of God, had to have faith. Yes, he prayed all night before choosing his disciples and yes, he obeyed by gathering the twelve whom God had provided for him. However, to look upon them, to see their backgrounds, on the surface they had very little potential for the journey ahead. Few would have predicted them to be a success. The thought of them working together or individually to teach, train, and lead others to change the world was beyond human hope. Jesus, the Son of God, had to have faith in his Heavenly Father's mission before he began to teach this eclectic group of men. Without God, this rugged, ragtag group would be a waste of time. In like manner, God has sent us those who, without his direction and intervention, would be an equally impossible task.

So, what spiritual qualities do we hope to instill in those we mentor and equip with the help of the Holy Spirit? Jesus reveals those qualities by contrasting the characteristics of his future equippers with the characteristics of those who would not be considered his disciples.

Blessed are you who are poor

Jesus began by saying, *"Blessed are you who are poor, for yours is the kingdom of God"* (Luke 6:20b NIV). Notice the confidence Jesus had in his Father when he presumed these men could be blessed at all, much less be a blessing to others. In addition, notice Jesus uses the word "poor". Most, if not all these disciples would have been considered poor after giving up their livelihoods and following Jesus. The only thing they did possess was their faith in Jesus and their willingness to believe the future could be different. They may not have fully understood what Jesus, the great equipper, was saying, but they believed in his leadership and his love and acceptance.

Through the Spirit, a new meaning of the word "poor" was revealed to Jesus' followers. He was not talking about them being poor as in having no money, but rather "poor" in desiring for the things this world has to offer. Those who do not follow Jesus try to find meaning in life through wealth, titles, the approval of people, and countless other disappointing means. But Jesus' future disciples/equippers had received Jesus' blessing. Although they did not understand all Jesus meant, they understood his promise that they would be blessed more than what this world had to offer if they followed him.

Jesus then addressed those who are rich in verse 24. Jesus said, *"But woe to you who are rich, for you have already received your comfort"* (Luke 6:24 NIV). He states that earthly riches will not bring lasting and eternal comfort. Jesus is not against people having riches, for these are a blessing if used in the right way. After all, there are those like Joseph of Arimathea who would provide a means for Jesus to be buried after his crucifixion. Nevertheless, Jesus did not want us to think what we could gain in this world could ever be greater than what we could gain in serving him. *"Blessed you who are poor, for yours is the kingdom of God"* (Luke 6:20b NIV).

Things this world has to offer are never enough. Jesus was equipping his disciples to be willing to be poor in this world, if need be, to be rich in the things of God.

Questions:

What traits would you hope a person would have if you were going to equip them?

What are some ways Jesus might guide you regarding how to equip a certain person?

How would you describe a person who is spiritually poor, and secondly, a person who is spiritually rich?

How might it be different to mentor and equip someone who is poor in a spiritual sense in comparison to someone who is rich in a spiritual sense? What would be some differences in relating and communicating with them?

In what ways have you sacrificed to be poorer in Spirit or closer to God?

Contemplate:

Although we may not want to do it, we must be willing to give up titles, money, friendship, etc., if God would ask us to do so.

Many things God will ask us to give up are not bad in themselves, but they will slow us down or distract us in accomplishing what is in our and God's best interest.

What God wants us to keep at this time in our lives is what we really need.

A Promise to the Hungry

Blessed are you who hunger now!

Next, Jesus says, *"Blessed are you who hunger now, for you will be satisfied"* (Luke 6:21 NIV). The word "hunger" resonated with the disciples. Recently, Jesus and his disciples had entered a house when suddenly a crowd gathered around the house. Although Jesus and his disciples were hungry, they were not able to eat (Mark 3:20 NIV). The disciples must have remembered how hungry they were. However, at this time Jesus was not talking about being hungry for food. Having an appetite for food is normal. Jesus was referring to being hungry for God's will to be done, while trusting him for our physical needs and satisfactions to be met. Life is more than what we eat or what we drink or what we wear (Matthew 6:31 NIV). Furthermore, to encourage us to trust him, Jesus said, *"For the pagans run after all these things, and your heavenly Father knows that you need them. But seek first his kingdom and his righteousness, and all these things will be given to you as well"* (Matthew 6:32-33 NIV).

People who are not intentional Jesus' followers will attempt to find fulfillment in everything this world has to offer besides trust in God. The ultimate result is spiritual starvation, misery, loss. The tragedy is that we, as Christians, can experience spiritual starvation by becoming so consumed with good things, even church things, that we have little time for the essential, that being our personal relationship with God. Jesus warns us by saying, "Woe to you who are well fed now, for you will go hungry" (Luke 6:25a NIV). On the other hand, Jesus promises his true followers, "Blessed are you who hunger now, for you will be satisfied" (Luke 6:21a NIV). What this world provides can never satisfy our deepest needs. It is always best to wait on and to trust God's timing and priorities.

Questions:

How is experiencing inappropriate desires different from experiencing holy desires?

Why does God allow inappropriate desires to enter our lives?

If you feel comfortable in sharing, how has God removed inappropriate desires from your life and introduced holy ones?

Contemplate:

Inappropriate desires can be like a fog that covers and distorts dangers ahead.

127

We do not leave inappropriate desires as much as we spiritually grow into new desires that are spiritually healthy and holy.

Spirit-led holy selflessness is God's gift to us in order to flee from evil.

A Promise to those who Weep

Blessed are you who weep now!

The third beatitude Luke shares is, *"Blessed are you who weep now, for you will laugh"* (Luke 6:21b NIV). It is obvious that there is much suffering in this world and there is much to weep over. Also, it is obvious, those who are Christ's followers will weep over things that non-believers will never understand or feel a need to weep over. The Holy Spirit illuminates the perceptions of Christians, and their hearts grow heavy because of seeing others reap the consequences of sin. It is sad to watch humankind struggle to be happy, while being unwilling to accept God's will which is the only means to achieve true and lasting happiness.

Jesus, in his humanity, understood the sorrow and weeping that humanity experiences, such as the death of a loved one. In John 11:35 (NIV) we find the shortest verse in the Bible which is blunt and to the point. The verse reads, *"Jesus wept"* (John 11:35 NIV). The verse reveals the raw emotion Jesus experienced when his friend Lazarus died. Some Jews who were present noticed Jesus' grief and said, *"See how he loved him"* (John 11:36 NIV). Then, as a lesson to all concerning our greatest sorrows, Jesus brought Lazarus back to life. Such action was significant because it was a foretaste of a time when we will know the power of resurrection and weep no more. Jesus not only wept in a way that all humans weep, but he also wept over what his followers would one day weep over. He wept over the spiritual lostness of humanity.

To me, one of the saddest and most moving moments in all of Scripture is when Jesus approached Jerusalem and began to weep. To many Jews of that day, Jerusalem was symbolic of the best God had to offer in this life. Jerusalem to them represented what God required and what humankind could expect from him. But that perception was wrong. Jerusalem symbolically may have represented the hope of tomorrow, but it was blind to Jesus' presence and mission. The One true hope that looked upon Jerusalem was weeping. Jesus said, *"If you, even you, had only known on this day what would bring you peace - but now it is hidden from your eyes"* (Luke 19:42 NIV). Matthew describes the scene with Jesus saying, *"O Jerusalem, Jerusalem, you who kill the prophets and stone those sent to you, how often I have longed to gather your children together, as a hen*

128

gathers her chicks under her wings, but you were not willing. Look, your house is left to you desolate" (Matthew 23:37-38 NIV).

Jesus prepared his disciples for the future by saying *"Blessed are you who weep now, for you will laugh"* (Luke 6:21b NIV). Jesus was aware of all the laughter and merriment that would take place by those who have never wept for lost humanity and the destructiveness of sin at his death. But they would end up weeping when their schemes would fail to bring the desired end. In Luke 6:25b NIV, Jesus said, *"Woe to you who laugh now, for you will mourn and weep."* Jesus was not opposed to laughter and having a good time, but he is opposed to not being emotionally and spiritually sensitive to the spiritual lostness of humanity.

In short, Jesus wanted his disciples to be willing to weep, if need be, over present suffering while being aware that the future will bring laughter and joy.

Questions:

As much as possible, explain the difference in grieving the loss of a Christian friend and grieving the loss of someone who does not know God?

Jesus was healthy emotionally. He truly loved and carried a burden for the lost world around him. However, he also cared for his own emotional wellbeing. To what extent should we, as his disciples, carry a burden for the lost and also be careful to care for our own emotional wellbeing? Do you think God expects us to live a balanced life? If so, what does that balance look like?

Contemplate:

We cannot be like Jesus without being about his mission of caring for lost people.

Jesus had more than a tear for the lost; he submitted himself to death on the cross for our salvation.

The obedient steps we take in sacrifice for Jesus are tears of the heart that are making their way to our eyes.

A Promise to those who are Hated

Blessed are you when men hate you!

In Luke 6:22 (NIV) we read, *"Blessed are you when men hate you, when they exclude you and insult you and reject your name as evil, because of the Son of Man."* Hate is a strong word. Someone who is hated is increasingly excluded, insulted, slandered. The final impact is that the hated person is seen as evil. These words from Jesus created great dissidence in the minds of the disciples. No one wants to be hated and certainly blessing would not flow out of words and actions of hatred. But Jesus said they do.

Before the words we read in Luke 6:20 (NIV) were spoken, the disciples had already experienced a mild degree of rejection from others. Remember, in Mark 2:16b (NIV), the Pharisees who saw Jesus eating with sinners and tax collectors asked the disciples, *"Why does he eat with tax collectors and 'sinners'"?* Later, in Mark 2:18b (NIV) some people asked, *"How is it that John's disciples and the disciples of the Pharisees are fasting, but yours are not?"* Pressure from the religious elite was already building against the disciples as they followed their new leader. The disciples no doubt were looking forward to the time in which those, who mistakenly thought evil of Jesus and this new movement, would turn and embrace Him and them as saviors. But in this passage Jesus paints a more challenging picture of the future for them. Persecution was coming. In the future the disciples would be hated even more. They would be excluded, personally insulted, and falsely accused. The "blessing" of being with Jesus would have to wait until a later time.

We know from history that in their early years of Christianity, the disciples were primarily persecuted by the religious leaders of that day. As they followed Jesus faithfully they experienced all the persecutions Jesus mentioned. Others, such as Paul, who came to follow Jesus later, would be persecuted in the same ways. In Acts 24:5-7 (NIV), we read that Paul was hated, rejected by the religious community he once loved, and was labeled not just as a Christian but as a Nazarene, which was a derogatory term at that time. Furthermore, he was often slandered and falsely accused. So how is a disciple to respond to this hatred and persecution?

Jesus stresses how we are to respond to hatred and persecution in Luke 6:27 (NIV). The answer is love. The pathway to blessing is to love those who hate us. Such love only comes from a heart of one who personally knows the depth of God's love. Of course, the perfect example of that love is found in the life of Jesus. When we listen closely to his instructions and follow in obedience, we will find blessing in the midst of hatred and persecution.

Questions:

Have you ever felt like you were tempted to hate someone?

You can love people in Christ but not "like" them as persons. In such a case, how do you negotiate the difference when trying to relate to them?

Contemplate:
What is an example of people who love others with the love of God but find it difficult to like them? How would those people show their love for those they didn't "like"?

Where to Begin

Jesus challenges the disciples and us to *"Love your enemies, do good to those who hate you, bless those who curse you, pray for those who mistreat you"* (Luke 6:25b NIV). As Jesus' disciples we must not only be willing to listen, but we must also be willing to love others, do good to others, bless everyone, and pray with a merciful attitude.

As mentioned earlier, the path of discipleship includes persecution. Most often the persecution grows in intensity as the disciple's life more closely resembles the life of Jesus. As growing disciples, often the greatest hurt experienced is from friends and family; those closest to us. Regardless of the intensity of the persecution, it is imperative that we continue to pray for our accusers.

In this passage, Jesus is equipping his future mentors and equippers for the challenges they would face in the world. However, their first experiences would come from within their own group – with each other. Likewise, the first and best school for church people to learn how to love and care for others is inside a small group. The experiences there will help them effectively respond redemptively to those who despise God and his Church.

There are a number of passages in the New Testament where the disciples practiced being redemptive in times of stress and misunderstanding. In Mark 8:32-33 (NIV), Jesus was sharing about his upcoming death, and Peter reacted by taking Jesus aside and rebuking him. Jesus responded by saying, *"Get behind me, Satan!" he said. "You do not have in mind the things of God, but the things of men"* (Mark 8:33 NIV).

The disciples were ordinary men who had not yet learned the humility Jesus wanted them to possess as leaders and mentors. In Mark 9:33b-34 (NIV), Jesus asked them, *"What were you arguing about on the road?" But they kept quiet because on the way they had argued about who was the greatest"* (among them).

Great battles against Satan outside the church are often first won inside the church. The preparation begins within the discussion and dynamics of a small group or class. Loving and redemptive encounters inside a small group or class can provide the strength and means to handle the persecution a disciple will face in the world.

131

How to Receive the Blessings

God has provided everything you need for this important ministry. In Him you already have his blessing and the mission of mentoring and equipping others to walk with Jesus. Just like Jesus, we need to say yes to what God has provided. It will be enough.

As Jesus' disciples we may live with many earthly wants and unfulfilled desires. Other people may not understand or accept our methods or lifestyle. And the result of our obedience to God may be personal hardship, rejection, and at times outright persecution.

But the reality is that as a disciple of Christ and a child of God we have access to all the resources of his kingdom. Those resources, allotted by the Holy Spirit, will bring peace out of chaos and joy out of loss. We just need to trust him.

It is wise to remember that today's obstacles are the seeds of tomorrow's blessings.

Keep your godly love fresh by remembering:

Blessed are the poor whose gold is kept in the heart of God.

Blessed are those who hunger for what only God can satisfy.

Blessed are those who weep over what makes God sad.

Blessed are those who are hated by the world in order to have the approval of God.

Be active:

"Rejoice in that day and leap for joy, because great is your reward in heaven. For that is how their fathers treated the prophets" (Luke 6:23 NIV).

While you are waiting to understand the greater depths of Jesus, simply *"Do to others as you would have them do to you"* (Luke 6:31 NIV).

Keep equipping! You will be blessed!

Lesson 4

The Journey of a Mentor and Equipper

Scripture:

"The angel of the Lord came back a second time and touched him and said, 'Get up and eat, for the journey is too much for you'" (1 Kings 19:7 NIV).

"And after the fire came a gentle whisper. When Elijah heard it, he pulled his cloak over his face and went out and stood at the mouth of the cave" (1 Kings 19:12b-13 NIV).

"Elijah was a man just like us. He prayed earnestly that it would not rain, and it did not rain on the land for three and a half years. Again he prayed, and the heavens gave rain, and the earth produced its crops" (James 5:17-18 NIV).

"Therefore encourage one another and build each other up, just as in fact you are doing" (1 Thessalonians 5:11 NIV).

Elijah – God's Prophet

Introduction:

This lesson introduces us to Elijah, one of the greatest prophets and mentors in all of Scripture. However, it will help us recognize some positive and negative tendencies we might have that would be like his that need to be avoided.

Both mentoring and equipping involve journeys of grace for both mentor and mentee. As we proceed on our journey of being a Christian, the Holy Spirit will teach us all things we need to know and warn us of shadowy caves where we need not dwell.

Let's begin as we consider the Journey of a Mentor.

A Journey of Recognizing Strengths and Weaknesses

Mentors are not perfect. They have weaknesses as well as strengths, spiritual scars as well as accomplishments, and spiritual goals that have not yet been realized. Earlier, in our first series on Fervent Prayer, we emphasized Elijah as a man of prayer. That is true. In this lesson we also want to consider a weakness he had as a mentor.

As life continues for mentors, like everyone else, they personally discover new weaknesses and new spiritual goals they will endeavor to accomplish. This writer once watched a well-known seasoned minister react to something that was said to him with outpouring anger that only lasted a few seconds, but the reverberations from his voice seemed to echo for some time.

All our mentors can be just as surprised as we are that they have not represented their God well in a particular circumstance. Some days all mentors and mentees must be humble and willing to say, *"I wish I had done better."* As mentors are striving to grow spiritually, we all need to extend mercy knowing we are all very human while genuinely endeavoring to be like Christ.

If you had been one of those young men in the School of the Prophets in Elijah's time and heard about his emotional and spiritual struggle, you would probably have felt sorry for him as well as disappointed that this hero of the faith allowed himself to momentarily be off balance in serving God. Further, if you would have been one of those young men and gave a second thought to Elijah's stumble, you would have realized how vulnerable we all can be when we are attempting to accomplishing great tasks for God.

This lesson on Elijah is a reminder that we should never view our mentors as perfect in their thoughts, will, and emotions. Mentors are not perfect any more than anyone else. They are merely sojourners who, along with us, are seeking to do God's will. The only perfect mentor in whom we can find no fault is Jesus.

Questions:

How would you have felt if a seasoned well-known pastor that you knew surprised you with a display of anger as mentioned above?

If appropriate, would you mind sharing about a time when you embarrassed yourself because your actions conflicted with your desired Christian witness?

If Christian mentors are not perfect in performance, why do we need them as mentors?

Contemplate:

Being a mentor is like being a parent. You give advice to your children according to the experience you have with the helpful guidance of the Holy Spirit.

To be an effective mentor or mentee under the leadership of the Holy Spirit requires a continual life of prayer.

A Journey of Prayer in Times of Strength and Weakness

Elijah experienced a day when several extraordinary miracles had occurred. He had challenged the 450 prophets of Baal, and the 450 prophets of Asherah who ate at Jezebel's table, to meet him at Mt. Carmel. It was on this mountain he commanded everyone to choose between serving the Lord God Jehovah or the god of Baal. The confrontation between the forces of good and evil continued throughout the day (1 Kings 18 NIV). At the end, the writer of 1 Kings is very clear, letting us know the Lord God Jehovah soundly won the confrontation. The scriptures reveal that the Prophet Elijah was used by God in a mighty way.

Soon, as revealed in 1 Kings 19, the excitement diminishes, and Elijah's victory began to be smothered by threats of retribution. Jezebel, the evil wife of Ahab, makes plans to kill Elijah. Hearing the threats, Elijah becomes fearful and runs for his life. When Elijah comes to Beersheba in Judah, he leaves his servant there and continues to forge ahead alone. Finally, he comes to a small broom tree, sits down under the tree, praying to die. Under the broom tree, Elijah continued to slide into a state of depression. In that state he forgot the miracles God had provided in the past and those he had just experienced.

If we are honest we can relate to Elijah when things don't go the way we want them to go. We can feel, like Elijah, that God has forsaken us and that we are on our own. Those who are close to us try to pull us out of our negativity but we are so consumed by our fear and depression that we fail to comprehend what our friends are saying to us. We, like Elijah, are only focusing on our fears.

In the story we see that the high emotions of that day and the physical strain is causing Elijah to fall asleep. Notice in the scripture that God did not scold Elijah for his exhaustion and discouragement, his prayer for death to come. God accepted him in his depleted condition. He does the same for us.

Questions:

Would you mind sharing one of the biggest miracles you have ever observed and personally experienced?

Have you ever noticed how Satan can tempt us after a great worship experience?
time of revival, or other anointed times? Is that because many assume Satan is not present at that time? What might be another reason?

Since Elijah struggled with loneliness, why do you think Elijah left his servant and went further into the desert?

Elijah appears to be a very private person. Could he pray better with or without his servant with him?

Jezebel threatened Elijah's life. When you are threatened with danger and emotionally shaken, how long does it take for you to begin to seriously pray?

According to Scripture, Elijah was more than a day's journey in the desert before he prayed. Why might it have taken him so long? How many days might you have to travel before you would seriously pray?

Are you more concerned about how much you work to accomplish spiritual tasks or how much you rest between those tasks?

Contemplate:

There is a difference in thinking "I need to pray" and seriously praying.

A Journey of Gratitude Concerning God's Mercy

Elijah is not living in rebellion against God. He is in the process of growing through human weakness to greater spiritual strength. God let Elijah fall asleep and later sent an angel to feed him. The angel awakened him and told him to eat. It is important to note, for God to provide food for Elijah was not anything new. Earlier in his ministry, Elijah would have starved if God had not sent ravens with food. Later, when he was hungry, there was the widow at Zarephath who suppled his need. Elijah, the great prophet and mentor, may have fallen into depression and was spiritually disoriented, but God's merciful hand was still providing for his needs.

After allowing Elijah to sleep, an angel came to him, awakened him, and spoke to him. The angel spoke with firmness and said, *"...Get up and eat"* (1 Kings 19:5b NIV). After eating, Elijah went back to sleep. When the angel came the second time, instead of speaking with such firmness, the angel spoke with divine empathy and compassion saying, *"...Get up and eat, for the journey is too much for you"* (1 Kings 19:7b NIV). God truly knows not just what we need physically, but how we need to hear the message. God's tone is always right for the situation.

Questions:

Would you share a time when God was merciful in a time of need?

For what reason might God tell a person, *"the journey is too much for you"* (1 Kings 19:7b NIV)?

Contemplate:

God nourishes us to give us strength for future service.

A Journey of Strength for God's New Direction (Mission)

"Strengthened by that food, he traveled forty days and forty nights until he reached Horeb, the mountain of God. There he went into a cave and spent the night" (1 Kings 19:8b-9 NIV). It is important here to note that forty days later Elijah, the strong miracle working mentor, is still not psychologically and spiritually as strong as he once was. He is still consumed in self-pity because of how he viewed his situation.

At the cave, God gave Elijah a life-changing lesson. God abruptly called Elijah's name and asked him, *"What are you doing here, Elijah?"* (1 Kings 19:9b NIV). Exposing his self-pity Elijah said, *"I have been very zealous for the Lord God Almighty...I am the only one left, and they are trying to kill me too"* (1 Kings 19:10 NIV). The Lord then asks Elijah to leave the cave and stand on the side of the mountain. (Sometimes we need to leave our caves so we can clearly see and hear from God.) Elijah is slow to obey and remains in the cave. Nevertheless, God sent a powerful wind that tore the mountain apart, but the Lord's new message did not come through the wind. Then there was an earthquake, but the Lord's new message did not come through the earthquake. Then there was a fire, but the Lord's new message did not come through the fire. The Scripture then says, *"And after the fire came a gentle whisper. When Elijah heard it, he pulled his cloak over his face and went out and stood at the mouth of the cave"* (1 Kings 19:12b-13 NIV).

The uniqueness of the moment obviously got his attention. Up to this point Elijah's ministry was characterized by big miracles and other nature-altering events. However, this time, the Lord did not speak through some staggering event. The Lord was teaching Elijah that his voice could be soft and gentle and still be powerful and effective. This prophet who had witnessed the awesome power of God was now witnessing the awesome whisper of God.

We are not told exactly why Elijah responded so quickly to the still small voice; however, I believe, because Elijah was a man of prayer, he recognized the Lord's presence within the whisper. That small voice, filled with the intimate and personal presence of God, must have drawn Elijah from the darkness of the cave to the openness of God's new message. By coming out of the cave, Elijah showed one of the most important traits for both a mentor or mentee – being teachable.

Next, it seems God wanted to clear up the confusion Elijah possessed concerning that he was the only one left who was faithful to God. Just like God might ask any of us who have been dwelling in some personal emotional and spiritual cave, God specifically called Elijah by name and asked him the second time, *"What are you doing here, Elijah"* (1 Kings 19:13b NIV)? Just as before, Elijah begins to tell his story again about being zealous for the Lord and how he is the only faithful one left. This time the Lord ignores Elijah's self-serving speech. It is amazing how our isolation in the caves of self-pity can alter and prejudice our testimonies.

Instead of responding to Elijah's comment directly, the Lord gives Elijah a new purpose and direction. His ministry will now be broader in scope. Elisha will anoint Hazael king over Aram and anoint Jehu king over Israel. Furthermore, Elijah will anoint Elisha to succeed him as prophet. Elisha will be Elijah's new mentee.

Who would have ever thought God could take an older despondent prophet, hiding in a cave, and give him such an exciting assignment. Who would have ever thought God would choose someone who had become so weak and discouraged to now go out and anoint others for future leadership. In a few years Elijah will die, but the divine strength that flows through him will reach far into the future.

Remember back in 1 Kings 19:14 (NIV) when Elijah gave his second pride-filled complaint to God about how the people were acting so badly? Remember when he complained that he alone was the only faithful prophet? Remember how God discarded what Elijah was saying, giving him a new assignment to anoint others for leadership? God was not going to allow Elijah to go on his new assignment without a better perspective of reality.

Elijah had no reason to be filled with self-pity or be discouraged when he felt he was all alone in doing God's work. Nor, in the future would he ever be able to feel as though he was all alone and no one else was faithfully serving God. In 1 Kings 19:18 (NIV), God said to Elijah, *"Yet I reserve seven thousand in Israel – all whose knees have not bowed down to Baal and all whose mouths have not kissed him."*

All mentors can become tired and feel lonely. In our humanness it is to become discouraged along the way. Renewal comes when we move beyond self-pity to an encounter with God. It is that encounter that God reveals the path for restoration. Elijah's new ministry plan changed the landscape of the government and propelled a new mentee by the name of Elisha to carry out twice as many miracles as the prophet of old.

Questions:

What might you say if God called you by name and asked, *"What are you doing here"* (1 Kings 19:13b NIV)?

What do you think life was like for Elijah as he lived in an emotional and spiritual cave?

Elijah developed a self-serving speech (1 Kings 19:14 NIV) that was ready when needed to explain his depressed attitude. Can you give an example of what another self-serving speech might sound like? Might God ignore it as well?

What are some of the reasons people feel like they are alone in ministry? What should they do when that feeling overwhelms them?

When was the last time you received a new assignment from God? Has he specifically told you to continue to do what you are doing? If so, how?

Privately answer this question. Who do you see as your next mentee?

Contemplate:

God has given me a life to share with someone else.

To live beyond your time, you must be connected to the lives of others.

When Elijah left this world, he left in a chariot of fire. More importantly, he left mentees who would become mentors for others for years to come...and for eternity.

Notes:

Section 5:

Authentic Relationships

Lesson 1

Authentic Relationships

Scripture:

"Finally, all of you, live in harmony with one another; be sympathetic, love as brothers, be compassionate and humble. Do not repay evil with evil or insult with insult, but with blessing, because to this you were called so that you may inherit a blessing" (I Peter 3:8-9 NIV).

"Above all, love each other deeply, because love covers over a multitude of sins. Offer hospitality to one another without grumbling. Each one should use whatever gift he has received to serve others, faithfully administering God's grace in its various forms. If anyone speaks, he should do it as one speaking the very words of God. If anyone serves, he should do it with the strength God provides, so that in all things God may be praised through Jesus Christ" (I Peter 4:8 – 11b NIV).

Introduction:

Our fifth core principle is Authentic Relationships. In this series of lessons, we will consider some of the basic components of Authentic Relationships.

Lesson 1: We will distinguish the difference between Authentic Relationships in General and Authentic Relationships in a Christian context. We will see how brothers and sisters are to live together in unity. Our focus will then see that the scope of authentic Christian relationships is not only to our families, but to anyone the Holy Spirit directs our way. Finally, we will delve into the topic of disagreements in the church.

Lesson 2: We will see that Living in Authentic Relationships is impossible without the help of the Holy Spirit, and see from Isaiah's prophecy how the Holy Spirit would affect Jesus' ministry. We will conclude with how the Holy Spirit prepares us for authentic relationships.

Lesson 3: We move from preparation to Maturing in Authentic Relationships. There is one challenge that every Christian will face and that is being willing to confront others. Also, we will see that we must be reconciled to God if we are going to mature in our walk with him. Within this lesson is a section on Characteristics of Authentic Christian Relationships.

Lesson 4: We close our series on Coming Together through Authentic Relationships. We will look at the lives of Peter, a Jew, and Cornelius, a Gentile: two worlds, yet one. We end with

Peter seeing a scattered church during his day; however, they were unified by the Cornerstone, Christ Jesus.

Authentic Relationships in General

Authentic relationships are based on people being sincere, genuine, and being themselves. However, we must remember people can be authentically good or bad depending on their character and motives. In either case, authentic relationships have something that binds two or more people together. This binding is the common interest, common need, and common goal of those in the relationship.

There can be many types of authentic relationships whether between business partners, teacher/student relationships, friends at work, etc. These various relationships may last a short time or a very long time depending on the needs of the people involved and the commitment to those needs.

Authentic relationships are not static, nor are they perfect due to many reasons. Here are just a few:
1) the people involved may be developing new opinions about what holds the individuals or group together, and they want to change the core purpose of the reason to be together.
2) those in the relationship may be making new commitments that threaten the time needed for the relationship's goals to be met.
3) as people may be changing through personal life's experiences, the priorities of their lives may have changed, and they no longer need the purpose of the relationship/group to be fulfilled. This is especially true when people go through developmental changes.

Nevertheless, because people change and are not perfect in relating to themselves or to others, their relationships are always changing and never perfect except in some measure of perfect intentions.

Questions:

Can you share an example when a friendship dissolved because of changing needs or interests? What was the length of the friendship and did the shift take place on your part or on the part of the other person?

Have you ever been part of a cluster of friends at church and felt like the relationships dissolved? Did you feel like your interest changed, or did change occur in the lives of others?

How might the experiences differ when relationships break up with those who are Christian believers or those who are not?

Is the process of healing more difficult to navigate for you when those in the cluster of people are Christian believers? or non-believers?

Contemplate:
What we gain in life's experiences from any relationship should always be used to build Christian character.

A book you may want to consider as you navigate through this series of Authentic Relationships is: *"Being Transparent with Yourself, God, and Others."* This book, written by *Susan M. Sims, is about being honest with where you stand in your relationships. This book will guide you in discussions and questions about places where you feel stuck. Honesty with yourself about where you are in life will start the journey to authentic relationships with yourself, God, and others.

*Susan Sims is our daughter, grew up as a pastor's kid, and realized as an adult just how important it is to be transparent with yourself, God, and others so authentic relationships can be healthy.

Authentic Relationships in a Christian Context

Trying to be authentic in relating with one another reminds me of a church I pastored where the church board and pastor made some serious attempts to relate well with each other through the years. A particular board member almost always called me by the name of Pastor. However, over the years, those other times were usually moments when the board had to make some important decision. Then it would happen. When he wanted to ask my opinion, he would look at me and softly refer to me as Brother Hicks. I never particularly cared for that name; however, on those few occasions, the name was especially meaningful, and it certainly got my attention in a positive way.

The term brother is frequently used throughout the Bible, and certainly applies to what is at the root of authentic relationships. I know in our present-day church culture, some people refer to their pastor as Pastor, Dr., Rev., or even by their first name, and all these names are certainly acceptable depending on the congregation. However, when we really need to relate authentically, we recognize, by the Spirit, just exactly who we have in common (Jesus), who we are with each other (brothers and sisters), and the task that holds us together (the Great Commission). We are brothers and sisters in Christ, authentically and relationally.

As brothers and sisters in Christ, we are equals. We may have different roles in Christian leadership and individual gifts to carry out ministries, but there is no difference in the amount of dedication each participant gives so ministry can continue. The combined relationships of all followers of Jesus have a purpose that connects us all. That purpose is to glorify God by endeavoring to live a life of Christlikeness, to carry out the works of God, such as the Great Commission, and to love others unconditionally as God has loved us. At the core of that connectiveness that holds us together is the activity of journeying together and walking together as the Body of Christ to glorify God. The attempt to build any relationship that does not include the Spirit of Christ can never function as an authentic Christian relationship.

Questions:

From your perspective, how do Christian relationships differ from non-Christian relationships?

How might God bless Christian relationships differently from non-Christian relationships? At what point might God's jealousy become engaged in the relationship, and how might that be experienced?

Contemplate:

Whether Christian or non-Christian, all relationships take time and energy that will draw us closer or move us further from God's purpose for our lives.

Brothers and Sisters in Christ

"How good and pleasant it is when brothers live together in unity" (Psalm 133:1 NIV)!

The Bible recognizes that Christians are brothers and sisters outside of being related by blood or natural family ties. The Psalmist wrote, *"How good and pleasant it is when brothers live together in unity"* (Psalm 133:1 NIV)! In the same context, the Psalmist says, *"For there the Lord bestows his blessing, even life forevermore"* (Psalm 133:3b NIV).

God planned this special ability to authentically relate eons ago. He began by allowing us to relate with him authentically. *"Praise be to the God and Father of our Lord Jesus Christ, who has blessed us in the heavenly realms with every spiritual blessing in Christ. For he chose us in him before the creation of the world to be holy and blameless in his sight. In love he predestined us to be adopted as his sons through Jesus Christ, in accordance with his pleasure and will"* (Ephesians 1:3-5 NIV).

We were all invited to be part of God's great adoption program, and to be capable of authentically relating through the Holy Spirit to him, as well as our Christian brothers and sisters. *"And you also were included in Christ when you heard the word of truth, the gospel of your salvation. Having believed, you were marked in him with a seal, the promised Holy Spirit, who is a deposit guaranteeing our inheritance until the redemption of those who are God's possession – to the praise of his glory"* (Ephesians 1:13-14 NIV). Because we have the Holy Spirit within us, we have the possibility to communicate as adopted brothers and sisters through authentic relationships.

Because of the term "brother" or "brethren" being used, I want to clear up any potential misunderstandings concerning the meaning of those terms and our application to authentic Christian relationships. The Scriptures never say or imply that only men should have what we are calling authentic Christian relationships, and that women are not given the privilege and joy of authentic Christian relationships. The idea of Brotherhood (which would include Sisterhood in our day) is viewed both in the Old Testament and New Testament. In the Old Testament, Israel was considered the Brotherhood (Zechariah 11:14 NIV), and in the New Testament the Believers, those believing in Christ, are considered the Brotherhood (I Peter 2:17 NIV).

The terms brothers or brethren are used multiple times in the New Testament. Sometimes the term is limited to men, and other times it includes both men and women. Any confusion can usually be cleared up by simply seeing if women are involved in the context of what is taking place. Obviously, most of the time, this is the case. Nevertheless, as Christ's followers, we must remember in all authentic Christian relationships *"there is neither Jew nor Greek, slave nor free, male nor female, for you are all one in Christ Jesus"* (Galatians 3:28 NIV). Jew, Greek, slave and free, male, and female are all expected to share and minister in a context of authentic Christian relationships. Simply put, the Body of Christ is one pulsating, active, and ever-expanding authentic relationship surrendered to God's purpose and will.

The Scope of Authentic Christian Relationships

The field or scope of authentic Christian relationships in which Christians are to work would include everyone the Holy Spirit leads us to at any given moment. This includes those the Holy Spirit is presently working with who have never committed their life to Christ (Prevenient Grace), those who have received forgiveness of their sins and are following Christ (Saving Grace), and thirdly, those who are already walking in the Spirit through God's Sanctifying Grace. All of us need to give and receive spiritual encouragement, or sometimes even gentle correction as we relate to one another.

As we are led by the Spirit to invite people to become followers of Christ, and as we are led by the Spirit to encourage and advise the brothers and sisters around us, we need to be sensitive to potential dangers in our own hearts. One of those spiritual dangers to avoid would be limiting those we are willing to minister to at any given time. For example, some people limit their ministries to their own family members. Jesus could have fallen into this relational trap but did not. The Scriptures say, *"While Jesus was still talking to the crowd, his mother and brothers stood outside, wanting to speak to him. Someone told him, 'Your mother and brothers are standing outside, wanting to speak to you.' He replied to him, 'Who is my mother, and who are my brothers?' Pointing to his disciples, he said, 'Here are my mother and my brothers. For whoever does the will of my Father in heaven is my brother and sister and mother'"* (Matthew 12:46-50 NIV).

In these Scriptures Jesus is not saying for his followers not to minister to their own families. He is saying that his ministry and our ministry includes more than our own families. Secondly, authentic Christian relationships are different than other relationships. Therefore, many people can have more in common with their spiritual brothers and sisters than those in their own biological families.

We all love our families and God loves them as well. However, the world wants to see what Christians look like as they relate not just to their families, but with the stranger whom they have never met. When they watch us relate to the stranger, surely some will respond as they did with Peter and John, *"...they were astonished and they took note that these men had been with Jesus"* (Acts 4:13b NIV).

147

Perhaps the greatest gift Jesus ever gave his family, besides dying on the cross, was the mental picture he left with them as he was dying. If a picture is worth a thousand words, that was surely an example of an authentic relationship between Jesus and his Father, and Jesus and those watching. For any family members watching, he authentically related to them with the words echoing from the past "...*I had to be in my Father's house*" (Luke 2:49b NIV).

My mother passed away many years ago. One of my most lasting memories I have of her is when, as a boy, she took me with her, drove across town, and spent an hour talking to a nonbeliever about Jesus. I remember the tone in her voice and how carefully she chose her words. We could have done something else that night, but she chose the finer thing, something I would never forget. If we want to leave something special for our children and other family members to remember us by, perhaps modeling what an authentic tone in our voice might be, and earnestly relating what Jesus can do for anyone would be a picture worth a thousand words.

Questions:
What is the difference in talking with someone in your immediate family about Jesus and someone in your extended family?

How might that differ than talking with a stranger about the importance of following Jesus?

If you could leave two memories in your child's mind, what would they be?

Contemplate:
Death is not as big of a tragedy as the lack of godly memories.

The Glory from Disagreements

One of the most exciting times in the life of brothers and sisters in the church is when they disagree. People who are not Christians may stake their claims and have a turf war like two animals in the wild. Christians recognize their disagreements and prayerfully gather around the throne seeking a solution so our reputation of being brothers and sisters will not be damaged. Many times, the presence of God is seen more when we disagree than when we sing our hymns of hallelujahs. People can sing songs of praise without authenticity, but they cannot seek God's will or protect our brothers and sisters without it.

Years ago, Mildred Bangs Wynkoop had just finished her book *"A Theology of Love: The Dynamic of Wesleyanism"*. She had been invited to visit Nazarene Theological Seminary and defend her positions among other very worthy professors. As a seminarian, I was especially interested in that important debate because I remembered sitting in a 7:00 a.m. class at Trevecca Nazarene College (now University) while she was writing and teaching her book. She would arrive in the classroom and, as one of the seven or eight students in the class, we would separate the moist mimeograph papers which represented the latest of her conclusions. On occasion, while teaching, she would interrupt herself and graciously ask the class, from a standpoint of Scripture, did we view things differently. Obviously, we were no match for her scholarliness. Yes, I had a real interest in how things would go when other scholars had an opportunity to share their views.

The pressure was not only on her but also on the other professors as they would debate. Could they have differences in opinion while appreciating each other with respect? Prior to the opening, and while students were gathering in, one student said, *"I am not here for the facts; I am here to feel the love."*

It isn't always easy to share differences in opinions while loving each other. But Jesus does when he talks to us and encourages us or corrects us. Today, I can still feel the dynamics that were in that large room. I can still remember the expressions on various faces. At times, there was tension but also, there was God's glory. I, too, was not there for the facts; I was there to feel the love between these brothers and this sister while they sought to better serve Jesus. I was not disappointed.

Authentic relationships are all about Christians being human while being anointed by the Spirit. If you want to see how much we love each other and experience God's glory, maybe attending a worship service would not be nearly as revealing as watching the grapes break and the new wine of the Spirit released when we disagree.

Questions:

For you, what is the most difficult aspect of disagreeing with a brother or sister in Christ?

If someone watched you in a disagreement with another Christian, what benefits would come to that person from the experience?

Contemplate:

Disagreements between two Christians is not a test of who is right, as much as a test of who is righteous.

Lesson 2
Living in Authentic Relationships

Scriptures:

"Do not be deceived: God cannot be mocked. A man reaps what he sows. The one who sows to please his sinful nature, from that nature will reap destruction; the one who sows to please the Spirit, from the Spirit will reap eternal life. Let us not become weary in doing good, for at the proper time we will reap a harvest if we do not give up. Therefore, as we have opportunity, let us do good to all people, especially to those who belong to the family of believers" (Galatians 6:7-10 NIV).

"So I say, live by the Spirit, and you will not gratify the desires of the sinful nature" (Galatians 5:16 NIV).

Introduction:

To live as human beings and aspire toward living and communicating in a context of Christian authentic relationships is impossible without the help of the Holy Spirit. Therefore, we need to look at how Jesus, in his humanity, was enabled to live and achieve such high expectations. We can never be as perfect as Jesus, but we can receive the Holy Spirit and allow the fruit of the Spirit to develop and grow within us. This fruit, or Spirit-filled qualities, should continue to grow more and more to mirror the type of authentic relationships Jesus would experience. Further, as the Body of Christ, we can come together as living stones and give both witness and example of our efforts in allowing Christ to work through us and create authentic relationships for his glory.

Let us begin with at least one way, while being human, Jesus was prepared and enabled by the Spirit to engage in authentic relationships.

Jesus' Preparation for Authentic Relationships

In the book of Isaiah, chapter 11, Israel was at one of its lowest levels as a nation and needed the help of God. Various kings had come and gone and, each time a new king came to the throne, the hope was "this would be the king to restore the Kingdom of Israel." For various reasons, flaws in character, and weaknesses in leadership, failure resulted. Trust and confidence that government leaders could restore Israel back to the Golden Years was all but gone. It was not until the last of the Davidic kings (of Judah) died in exile that the emphasis changed in realizing what was needed; a future Messiah to fulfill Israel's needs.

Isaiah was inspired to make a list of godly Spirit-filled qualifications the Messiah would need to possess to truly meet the needs of humanity. Obviously, having these qualifications would contribute toward working within authentic relationships. These qualifications (listed below) are prophetic of those the Messiah would have when he came. Yes, Jesus would need these qualities for his work, but the Body of Christ would need them as well, and he would later share them with us according to our needs.

According to Isaiah's prophecy, there are seven ways the Holy Spirit would affect Jesus' ministry. First the passage will be given and then some brief comments on a breakdown of the passage.

"The Spirit of the Lord will rest on him – the Spirit of wisdom and of understanding, the Spirit of counsel and of power, the Spirit of knowledge and of the fear of the Lord – and he will delight in the fear of the Lord" (Isaiah 11:2-3a NIV).

"The Spirit of the Lord will rest on him" – the ability to rule and govern while human
"the Spirit of wisdom" – the ability to make the right decisions
"the Spirit of understanding" -- spiritual discernment
"the Spirit of counsel" -- the ability to guide others
"the Spirit of power" -- to take control such as casting out evil spirits
"the Spirit of knowledge" -- having an awareness of the Holy Spirit's actions and movements
"the Spirit of fear of the Lord" -- being sensitive to obey the purpose and will of God.

Some have referred to these characteristics as the 'Fruits of the Spirit of the Old Testament', and others have referred to these as the 'Gifts of the Spirit of the Old Testament'. Nevertheless, in this Messianic prophecy, we see that Jesus would possess these supernatural characteristics when the Spirit would descend on him. Later, John witnessed the Spirit's coming on Jesus and spoke of the event by saying, *"...I saw the Spirit come down from heaven as a dove and remain on him. I would not have known him, except that the one who sent me to baptize with water told me, 'The man on whom you see the Spirit come down and remain is he who will baptize with the Holy Spirit.' I have seen and I testify that this is the Son of God"* (John 1:32a-34 NIV).

The good news is that the same Spirit would come to all humankind on the day of Pentecost. In Jesus' humanity, he was an example that we, too, would receive the anointing of the Holy Spirit. The result of our receiving the Holy Spirit would not only lead to having the gifts of the Spirit as we needed them, but all the fruit of the Spirit, which we will discuss in the next section.

Once again, without the fruit of the Spirit, we would not be capable of having godly authentic relationships.

Questions:

Israel gave up on having an earthly king to solve their problems. What things did you give up on and later found your need met in Christ?

Before your conversion, if you would have made a list of what qualities a Savior would need to meet your personal needs, what qualities would have been on your list?

If you are not a Christian, what characteristics in a Savior do you feel are a must for you to accept Christ as your personal Savior?

Since Jesus was born with no sin in his life, why do you think he would need to be anointed with the fruit of the Holy Spirit?

How might Jesus have felt differently after he was anointed with the Spirit? What changes in his life do you think he experienced?

Isaiah made his list about a coming Messiah and prophesized Jesus' anointing approximately 700 years before it occurred. Except for prophecies from the Bible, do you know of anyone else down through history who has prophesized or predicted any event with such accuracy?

If someone prophesized about your future 700 years from now, what might that person say?

Contemplate:

Unlike us, Jesus did not need to be cleansed before he was empowered by the Holy Spirit.

The more we wrestle against the Holy Spirit, the more we injure ourselves and others.

Any life we live without the Holy Spirit is never the "Good Life" God intended.

Our Preparation for Authentic Relationships

Years ago, I had eaten lunch and was driving back to the office. Yes, I was driving the speed limit and driving appropriately. I took a right turn onto a four lane, and I did not see anyone coming around a curve behind me. Then suddenly a car was behind me that was speeding. Evidently, he was in a hurry and the speed limit was not fast enough for him.

He began honking his horn. I did not respond. He then came up close to my back bumper and was continuing to honk his horn. My car windows were tinted dark enough so he could not see me, but now he was so close I could see him as he was leaning over his steering wheel shouting inappropriate words. I kept driving normally, and he kept honking for perhaps half a mile. Then he hurried around me where he continued to find others to exercise his frustrations on.

I mentioned I could see him, but he could not see me. The fact is, he had no idea I was his pastor driving that car in front of him, and I had no idea he could drive so fast without both hands on the steering wheel.

The next Sunday I began the service with *"This is the day the Lord has made..."* (Psalm 118:24a NIV). He was present and had been a regular attender for several years. We shared our normal greetings at the end of the service, and I did not say anything that would embarrass him. The next year he asked to be in one of my small groups, and I agreed that would be a good idea. Several months into the class, the subject we were going to discuss concerned following the Spirit's leading. The class continued for over a year, and, over a period of time, he made some real changes in his life. His progressions were evident as he moved from experiencing God's prevenient grace, saving Grace and later sanctifying grace. He never knew I had watched him at one of his weak moments. Having experienced the fruit of the Spirit while driving would have benefited him greatly, especially the fruit called 'self-control'.

I am not sharing this story to make fun of someone's struggles; however, I am sharing this because we all can remember a time our actions would have been different if we had received and were exercising the fruit of the Spirit. Secondly, I share this story to remind us how God has watched all of us during such times and loved us unconditionally.

If you are ever going to have authentic Christian relationships with others, there are some things in your life that will have to be discarded and others added. Paul, in Galatians 5:19-26 (NIV), gives a list of what he refers to as acts of the sinful nature. Then he gives a list of good qualities that he refers to as the fruit of the Spirit. It is obvious that the acts of the sinful nature will destroy godly authentic relationships, and the fruit of the Spirit will build true authentic relationships.

As we have already seen, Jesus was anointed by the Spirit for his work of ministry. He could never have dealt with the relationship issues he was confronted with without having the fruit of the Spirit active in his life.

The Spirit wants to help us as well. Paul contrasts ways our lives will be drastically affected if we walk according to the flesh as opposed to according to the Spirit. Walking according to the flesh brings personal pain to us and will seriously damage our relationship with others, especially our friends who want to follow God. The fruit of the Spirit is to replace the corruptive poisons of the flesh. As we walk in the Spirit, spiritual health returns and Satan's poisons cannot survive.

We not only need the fruit of the Spirit to build and maintain authentic relationships with others, but we also need the fruit to have an ongoing authentic relationship between God and ourselves. John, on the island of Patmos, could not have lived with God relationally or even himself spiritually without the Holy Spirit.

Paul lists the things we need to have discarded, calling them "the acts of the sinful nature." He describes them when he says, *"The acts of the sinful nature are obvious: sexual immorality, impurity and debauchery; idolatry and witchcraft; hatred, discord, jealousy, fits of rage, selfish ambition, dissensions, factions and envy; drunkenness, orgies, and the like"* (Galatians 5:19-21a NIV). Then Paul speaks directly and says, *"I warn you, as I did before, that those who live like this will not inherit the kingdom of God"* (Galatians 5:21b NIV).

Paul also lists the things we need to receive from the Holy Spirit and calls them "the fruit of the Spirit." His descriptions and comments are, *"But the fruit of the Spirit is love, joy, peace, patience, kindness, goodness, faithfulness, gentleness and self-control. Against such things there is no law. Those who belong to Christ Jesus have crucified the sinful nature with its passions and desires. Since we live by the Spirit, let us keep in step with the Spirit. Let us not become conceited, provoking and envying each other"* (Galatians 5:22-26 NIV).

Nonbelievers may see the experiences of the sinful nature and the experiences of the fruit of the Spirit as competing against each other and, in quick judgement, conclude the sinful nature has more appeal and will give them more personal enjoyments. However, let's consider the comparison. After all, when Paul made his lists, he was comparing them so everyone could see the results.

If the acts of the sinful nature and the fruit of the Spirit are competing for our attention, the acts of the sinful nature draw us toward fleshly **pleasures** that ultimately lead to fleshly **chaos** that lead to fleshly **torment**. Left unchecked they finally destroy our personhood that Christ died for.

The fruit of the Spirit provides a remedy for our transitional pain through times of adjustment. The fruit of the Spirit supplies love, joy, and peace to replace our addiction to fleshly pleasures. The Spirit calms our complicated and **chaotic lives** with patience, kindness, and goodness. The Spirit stabilizes our **tormenting uncertainty** with gentleness, faithfulness, and self-control.

The pleasures of the flesh are not lasting pleasures, they are rather frantic attempts to find life more abundant. And the fruit of the Spirit is not an imitation fruit to study, observe, and then place back on a shelf. The fruit of the Spirit is alive and pulsating with energy. The pleasures of the flesh have now been overcome by a greater spiritual pleasure. The fresh breath we breathe is more than thin air. The breath that settled troubled waters and breathed an anointing on Jesus has now blown upon us. The same Spirit that enabled Jesus is now ours as well.

Families have a resemblance in their DNA; and sharing with Jesus, the fruit of the Spirit reveals our likenesses. The fleshly chaos that once thrived in our sinful natures now has no room to think, no plans to make, and no retaliations to act upon. The only things that remain are common temptations, like weights for us to resist, and like tests to grow our characters. Like Israel, we needed more than a leader, we needed a Messiah anointed with the Holy Spirit.

Love joy peace

The first three characteristics of the Spirit-filled life alone would be enough to send us to church. As humans, we were meant to express love, celebrate joy, and bathe in peace. The ancient world considered having personal peace as being alone, independent, and safe from others. Many today have gone back to those ancient models by refraining from worship services, distancing themselves from small groups, and attempting to avoid authentic relationships. However, peace, as a fruit of the Spirit, included experiencing peace with others.

Peace in the New Testament included corporate peace. This includes but is different than individual peace because this is more peace than one person can contain. When peace, as a fruit of the Spirit, came in a corporate way, the only way to experience it was to find a church, a small group, or meeting with other Christians in the context of authentic relationships. We must seek the precious peace of being alone with God, but we must also enjoy the beauty of peace that comes when two or more are gathered together. When the angels announced peace on earth, they came as a choir.

Questions:

What are examples of how acts of the sinful nature destroy godly authentic relationships?

Why would people be hesitant to be freed from the acts of the sinful nature?

Are the acts of the sinful nature that involve sexual immorality any worse than others such as hatred, discord, fits of rage, and envy?

Which one of the following fruits of the Spirit made the greatest effect on your life: love, joy, peace, and why?

Which one of the following fruits of the Spirit made the greatest effect on your life: patience, kindness, goodness, and why?

Which one of the following fruits of the Spirit made the greatest effect on your life: gentleness, faithfulness, self-control, and why?

If you were to witness to someone about which fruit of the Spirit made the greatest difference in your authentic relationships, which one would it be, and why?

Contemplate:

For the fruits of the Spirit to grow, they must have the nourishment of prayer and regularly receiving truth from the Word of God.

Concerning the progress of your fruits of the Spirit, keep your eyes on your own development and not the development of others.

We receive all the fruit of the Spirit at once, but some fruit matures and develops more quickly than others.

It Is the Holy Spirit's job to mature and develop each fruit; it is our job to keep up and walk with the Spirit.

Lesson 3

Maturing in Authentic Relationships

Scripture:

"For where two or three come together in my name, there am I with them" (Matthew 18:20 NIV).

"Above all, love each other deeply, because love covers over a multitude of sins" (I Peter 4:8 NIV).

Introduction:

The Scriptures are full of acknowledgments that God desires and expects individual Christians and entire churches to live in unity and harmony. This is an ongoing challenge, and a place for Satan to continually work. To counteract the work of Satan, we must be willing to learn skills to form, shape, and maintain authentic relationships. One of those skills is confronting people. Also, we will look at some characteristics of authentic relationships, and, before we conclude our lesson, we will consider the foundation of all authentic relationships, which is being reconciled to God.

Be Willing to Confront

Confronting is one of the most beneficial exercises in the church as we seek to mature in authentic relationships, and yet it can be one of the hardest for some people to do. Confronting will eliminate places where Satan wants to divide those in the church and in small groups. Confronting is easier for some people, and they really must spend time in prayer before deciding to confront to be certain they are in God's will. On the other hand, confronting is very difficult for others and, as they pray before confronting, they need to ask for courage.

All Christians should be lovers of divine peace. However, the idea that if we are going to be like Jesus in the church, that we must say nothing, must not communicate our feelings, and must never confront others, is a half-truth at best. Certainly, Jesus allowed people to treat him in horrific ways when it was for the glory of God. But when working with his disciples and building his church, he was open and direct. He loved them enough to correct them as needed. For us to be like Jesus, we must follow the leading of the Spirit and, after asking for wisdom, be willing to confront or not confront the person, as the Spirit leads.

As a pastor for many years I understand that one of the most important things to teach is when and how to confront others, under the direction of the Spirit. To confront one another is to say, "our relationship is important to me, and if something is wrong, I want to make it right." I have pastored one church for thirty-two years and taught small groups for more than forty years. Loving and appropriate communication is an essential ministry skill. Not to communicate or be engaged in learning to communicate, will ultimately destroy a marriage, and suffocate the breath of the Spirit as he works through either a marriage or a church.

The need to confront was a major concern and essential exercise for God's people even during New Testament times. In Matthew 18:20 (NIV) we read, *"For where two or three come together in my name, there am I with them."* So often we think of this Scripture when we want to gather others around us to pray for some special need, or we remind others in worship that God is with us because two or three are gathered together. Both thoughts are true. However, if we look at the more specific context of the verse, we see Matthew 18:15-20 (NIV) is in reference to confronting and solving a problem. Specifically, the passage has to do with a Christian who has sinned against you and hurt you. The broader principle presented here is to present what you should do if a relationship has been damaged. Matthew instructs us to go to the brother and discuss the matter with them directly, with the intent to preserve the relationship and solve the problem. If that discussion does not resolve the problem then take one or two others with you the next time (those who can see both sides of the issue) and seek a resolution. Then Matthew says, if that fails, get the opinion of the entire church. At this point, it is critical to realize the writer is thinking in the context of a house church, which may be only seven or eight people. Matthew then says if the brother who has harmed you is not willing to restore the relationship to a Christ-centered relationship, you should eliminate yourself from the relationship because there is not a willingness to solve the problem.

Let me say this again. Jesus wants every relationship in the church to be an authentic Christian relationship. Therefore, we have an obligation to go and confront as the Spirit leads us to do so. Going back to Matthew 18:20 (NIV) we read, *"For where two or three come together in my name, there am I with them."* In this passage Jesus is letting us know, if we are willing to obey the Spirit's direction to go confront and, if we are willing to go in Jesus' name to accomplish his purpose and not our own, he will be with us.

Some suggestions or tips when confronting:

When you meet with the person, keep the meeting short. This will assist those in the meeting to remember exactly what was discussed, what was agreed as to the problem, what were the existing opinions of those involved, and the concluding actions that need to be taken.

Do not attack the person. Attack the problem.

Only handle one or two problems at your meeting. Do not discuss other problems that have occurred in the past unless they relate to the present discussion.

Open and close the meeting with prayer and an attitude of love and respect for the person.

Realize you are there to solve a problem so it will not be repeated, not to win an argument.

Take a deep breath and breathe!

The section we just finished might have been a little uncomfortable for you, especially if you have difficulty in confronting. Also, we must remember, if we are going to truly have an authentic relationship with someone inside or outside of the church, there are certain characteristics that need to be part of that relationship.

Let's take a look

Some Characteristics of Authentic Christian Relationships

Authentic Relationships **risk our own safety** for the sake of the brethren.
   "This is how we know what love is: Jesus Christ laid down his life for us. And we ought to lay down our lives for our brothers" (I John 3:16 NIV).

Authentic Relationships require **discernment.**
   "They are from the world and therefore speak from the viewpoint of the world, and the world listens to them. We are from God, and whoever knows God listens to us; but

whoever is not from God does not listen to us. This is how we recognize the Spirit of truth and the spirit of falsehood" (I John 4:5-6 NIV).

Authentic Relationships assume everyone **needs** their own **personal time** to develop spiritually.
"Make it your ambition to lead a quiet life, to mind your own business and to work with your hands, just as we told you, so that your daily life may win the respect of outsiders and so that you will not be dependent on anybody" (1 Thessalonians 4:11-12 NIV).

Authentic Relationships are models of **purity**.
"For God did not call us to be impure, but to live a holy life" (I Thessalonians 4:7 NIV).

Authentic Relationships exercise **unconditional love**, even to our brothers and sisters.
"My brothers, if one of you should wander from the truth and someone should bring him back, remember this: Whoever turns a sinner from the error of his way will save him from death and cover over a multitude of sins" (James 5:19-20 NIV).

Authentic Relationships require us to **love as Jesus loves.**
"My command is this: Love each other as I have loved you" (John 15:12 NIV).

Authentic Relationships assume we **love one another.**
"Dear friends, let us love one another, for love comes from God. Everyone who loves has been born of God and knows God. Whoever does not love does not know God, because God is love" (I John 4:7-8 NIV).

Authentic Relationships assume God's **love** is made **complete** in us.
"Dear friends, since God so loved us, we also ought to love one another. No one has ever seen God; but if we love one another, God lives in us, and his love is made complete in us" (I John 4:11-12 NIV).

Authentic Relationships assume we **love others** and **serve them** as God has taught us.
"Now about brotherly love we do not need to write to you, for you yourselves have been taught by God to love each other. And in fact, you do love all the brothers throughout Macedonia. Yet we urge you, brothers, to do so more and more" (I Thessalonians 4:9-10 NIV).

Authentic relationships assume we feel a **responsibility to care** and **act** on the behalf of others.
"What good is it, my brothers, if a man claims to have faith but has no deeds? Can such faith save him? Suppose a brother or sister is without clothes and daily food. If one of you says to him, 'Go, I wish you well; keep warm and well fed,' but does nothing about his physical needs, what good is it? In the same way, faith by itself, if it is not accompanied by action, is dead" (James 2:14-17).

Authentic Relationships require our **obeying Jesus' teachings.**
> *"Jesus replied, 'if anyone loves me, he will obey my teaching. My Father will love him, and we will come to him and make our home with him'"* (John 14:23 NIV).

Authentic Relationships experience God's **peace** and **holy** presence with others.
> *"Make every effort to live in peace with all men and to be holy; without holiness no one will see the Lord. See to it that no one misses the grace of God and that no bitter root grows up to cause trouble and defile many"* (Hebrews 12:14-15 NIV).

Authentic Relationships involve **individual peace** for those in the relationship.
> *"Peace I leave with you; my peace I give you. I do not give to you as the world gives. Do not let your hearts be troubled and do not be afraid"* (John 14:27 NIV).

Questions:
Which three characteristics spoke to you the most and why?

Which characteristic would you like to be demonstrated in your church more?

Contemplate:
My experiences with God have given me the answer to someone's problem.

Be Reconciled to God

Background Reading: II Corinthians 5:11-20 NIV.

Scripture:
> *"So from now on we regard no one from a worldly point of view. Though we once regarded Christ in this way, we do so no longer. Therefore, if anyone is in Christ, he is a new creation; the old has gone, the new has come! All this is from God, who reconciled us to himself through Christ and gave us the ministry of reconciliation: that God was reconciling the world to himself in Christ, not counting men's sins against them. And he has committed to us the message of reconciliation. We are therefore Christ's ambassadors, as though God were making his appeal through us. We implore you on Christ's behalf: Be reconciled to God"* (II Corinthians 5:16-20 NIV).

In II Corinthians 5, Paul talks about "reconciliation" which involves the act of restoring relationships. We all have had to mend relational fences with others. Sometimes the fault was ours, and sometimes the crack that formed in the relationship was the fault of others. Nevertheless, the most important relationship we will ever have to be concerned about is our reconciliation with God. In addition, if we are going to be Christians and participate in authentic relationships, we must become skilled at enabling our brothers and sisters to be reconciled relationally not only with God, but with themselves and others.

There is no doubt that Paul had a great appreciation for authentic relationships. From his writings we see that, concerning spiritual matters, he was very observant and wanted everyone to be in the process of maturing spiritually. If Paul was alive today and attended your small group, church, or just walked up as you were meeting with some Christian friends, what might have been some of his thoughts as his analytical mind observed the meeting? No one can imagine all the possibilities, but the following Scripture passages reveal his thoughts concerning those at Corinth and their past, present, and future authentic relationships. It is also appropriate for us to consider the past, present, and future of those in our authentic relationships as we join them in fulfilling God's purposes. If Paul was to speak to us today about authentic relationships, I believe he would begin by saying, get beyond the failures of the past.

Get over the past – (II Corinthians 5:11-16 NIV)

Everyone in authentic relationships needs to get over the spiritual failures of their own past. Also, they should allow others to be released from their past. Any tendency to permanently label each other, regardless of who they are in relationship to you, will not allow them to begin anew. Those who have always appeared to be faithful to the Church and God, such as an elder brother, in contrast to the prodigal son, can be falsely labeled as easily as those whose lives were as the prodigal son. The elder brother could be thought of as aloof, prideful, and having a "better than others" attitude. The prodigal might be thought of as a reckless person who does not value spiritual faithfulness. Nevertheless, the people in both examples are as sinful as the other. Both became deceived by Satan in different ways. As far as we know, Adam and Eve never partied the night away as the Prodigal, but their sin and influence still wrecked what was holy. Therefore, we must get over our past and enable others to get over theirs as well.

In II Corinthians 5:11-16 NIV, Paul begins by asking those in the church at Corinth to take pride in his ministry. To do so, they would need to view things differently from the way they had in the past. In this world, people normally take pride in what is outward rather than what is from the heart. The focus can be on the clothes people wear or the education they have achieved. In former times, those at Corinth had been this way. Now, Paul wants them to get over the way they have been thinking and to begin to look at his heart if they want to see spiritual success. Paul's ministry originated in his heart. He did not want anything to take the focus off what God had done in his life. Paul's life had been changed.

Paul then explains further why reconciliation was needed. Some may have felt they were the exception and did not need to be brought back into relationship with God. However, everyone was out of relationship with God. Speaking of Christ, Paul says, *"...one died for all, and therefore all died"* (II Corinthians 5:14b NIV). Paul is letting them know Christ would not have died for everyone, unless everyone needed it. When we are involved with other people, in groups or as individuals, everyone needs God. Everyone needs to be restored.

Further, those who are restored to an authentic relationship with God through Christ, *"...should no longer live for themselves but for him who died for them and was raised again"* (II Corinthians 5:15b NIV). One key thing all people in authentic relationships have in common is they no longer live for themselves. The bias toward only self-interest has been taken away, and now we have room in our hearts, not only for God, but for others in the relationship.

Paul has emphatically said to every person, including those in authentic relationships, since we have been reconciled by God and our relationship with him has been restored, be willing to leave the past. Individually, we should not think about things from our past that will cloud our present relationship with God. Furthermore, if you are in a small group, don't think about things in other people's past that may cloud your relationship with God or them. People are trying to get beyond their past, and you should as well. Your relationship with God has been restored. Their relationship with God has been restored. To focus on what you were or did, or what they were or did, will only inhibit the development of the new authentic relationship that God is presently creating.

Since you have been reconciled in your relationship with God and with others, leave the past behind.

Be active in the present (II Corinthians 5:16 – 18 NIV)

Paul transitions from the past to the present as he says, *"So from now on we regard no one from a worldly point of view"* (II Corinthians 5:16a NIV). This statement naturally raises a question of "why", and verse 17 gives the answer - *"Therefore, if anyone is in Christ, he is a new creation; the old has gone, the new has come"* (II Corinthians 5:17 NIV)!

As Christians, we celebrate together that we now have more in common in the new life together than we had in the past. The work of the Holy Spirit has enabled us to share many basic concerns, to rejoice with those who rejoice, and mourn with those who mourn. We now, in Christ, have spiritual unity, and we never want it broken. If our relationship would be broken, we would all weep, and the authentic relationship of the group would be shattered.

We live in the present with a sensitivity that the Spirit's agenda is our first concern. When necessary, we share with others our concerns and, with love, gently move them toward correction. In moving toward correction, we don't confront harshly, but rather approach one another in love, with compassion and understanding from the Spirit. This same Spirit that filled hearts at Pentecost, guides the conversation so the objective of reconciliation is always in sight.

We know the "why" that all of this has taken place. *"All this is from God, who reconciled us to himself through Christ..."* (II Corinthians 5:18a NIV).

Create a new future (II Corinthians 5:19b-21 NIV)

The future can only be changed through Spirit-filled authentic relationships. The Jewish religious structure was well organized and leaders well trained. However, in all their searching, they never came up with the right plan of reconciliation. It would take God, who knew all about authentic relationships, to send his Son to reconcile the world. It would take the guidance of the Holy Spirit to teach us how to be authentic and be true friends with one another.

Like the Corinthians, our group of friends and builders of the New Kingdom has received the next step for God's plan - *"...he has committed to us the message of reconciliation. We are therefore Christ's ambassadors, as though God were making his appeal through us"*. (II Corinthians 5:19b-20a NIV).

It is a real honor to be an ambassador and represent a king to some distant country. Likewise, it is a real honor for our group of friends who have living in authentic relationships with each other to be ambassadors for Christ. It's incredible that God would trust us with such a task. But he has. Your little group is included in the great reconciliation movement of God. He reconciled us and we are called to be his ambassadors!

What will we say to others as we go out to share the ministry of reconciliation? The words we use may be different, but the meaning is the same. *"We implore you on Christ's behalf: Be reconciled to God"* (II Corinthians 5:20b NIV). To those without Christ, we will say, *"We implore you on Christ's behalf: Be reconciled to God"* (II Corinthians 5:20b NIV). Likewise, to those in some group of friends meeting in Christ's name, who have never felt the peace and joy of authentic relationships, we say, *"We implore you on Christ behalf: Be reconciled to God"* (II Corinthians 5:20b NIV).

Questions:

As Christians, what are some ways we can guard against focusing on our spiritual failures and turn our focus to a new life that has been reconciled to God?

For those participating in a small group, what are some ways we can remind and encourage others that they are restored both to God and also to the small group's authentic relationships?

What are ways a prodigal son and an elder brother can be restored through relating to one another authentically?

What are indicators that a person has truly been restored to God and has an authentic relationship with him?

After one is reconciled to God, what is the process of becoming reconciled to those in a small group or church?

As Christians, what indicators might be in our lives that would reveal to others that we are Christ's ambassadors?

How did you become part of an authentic relationship with another Christian and what was it like?

Contemplate:

As Christians, God has forgotten our past; now it is our turn.

You can be forgiven in a moment of time; however, for a lifetime, you may have moments of shame because of your past.

Lesson 4

Coming Together through Authentic Relationships

Scripture:

Read Acts 10:1-48, before coming to the session.

"Then Peter began to speak: 'I now realize how true it is that God does not show favoritism but accepts men from every nation who fear him and do what is right'" (Acts 10:34-35 NIV).

"As you come to him, the living Stone..." (I Peter 2:4a NIV).

"Live such good lives among the pagans that, though they accuse you of doing wrong, they may see your good deeds and glorify God on the day he visits us" (I Peter 2:12 NIV).

Come now, let us reason together
Isaiah 1:18a NIV

Introduction:

"'Come now, let us reason together,' says the Lord. 'Though your sins are like scarlet, they shall be as white as snow; though they are red as crimson, they shall be like wool. If you are willing and obedient, you will eat the best from the land; but if you resist and rebel, you will be devoured by the sword.' "For the mouth of the Lord has spoken" (Isaiah 1:18-20 NIV).

I remember, many years ago, talking with an elderly lay gentleman who had attended a church that had grown over the years to be a large prominent church in that city. While visiting, my curiosity got the best of me concerning the size of the present congregation, and I asked the gentleman this question: "Has this church always been large with attractive ministries and Spirit-led services?"

He looked at me and said, "No, it hasn't always been like this." He then shared with me the following story. He said he had always attended that church since a child, and then began to reminisce more. He told how it was once a relatively small church and there were basically two factions in the church. When people came to church, they would sit on the side 'their leader' was sitting. It was like that for several years. Also, when new people began to attend, there were attempts to persuade them to be loyal to one faction or the other.

One day a new pastor came to town and saw what he was up against. So, the only thing he knew to do was preach about unconditional love. After a couple of weeks, everyone knew when they came to church the subject of unconditional love was expected. This went on for months, and close to a year.

Then this elderly man recalled being a teen and present on a particular Sunday. Like others, he, too, knew what the sermon theme would be for the morning. By now, some had tired of the continuous emphasis, but were waiting to see if those sitting on the other side of the congregation would give in. As the story progressed about those teen years, tears began to carve paths down the elderly man's cheeks. He explained that, after that Sunday, the church was never the same. Once again, the pastor preached on unconditional love. At the close of the service, he stepped back from the pulpit and gave what seemed like one more normal invitation. But this invitation would not be normal because the key influencer for the left side of the congregation moved out from his seat and made his way to the furthest left-hand corner of the altar near the wall. Then to everyone's surprise, the other key influencer on the right side of the congregation moved from his seat and knelt at the furthest corner on the right side of the altar near the opposite wall. Seemingly, one man knelt on the left representing his side of the church, and the other man the opposite side. Neither man knew the other one had gone to the altar. The pastor stood at the pulpit and began to lead in prayer.

Suddenly, both men looked up from the altar at the same time and saw each other. Immediately they stood up, ran to each other and, meeting at the center of the sanctuary, began to hug and ask forgiveness. Next, people began moving from their seats, crossing the aisles hugging and asking forgiveness.

The church was never the same after that Sunday when two men submitted their personal wills to God, and the Holy Spirit was given freedom to act. A few weeks later, the church held a revival. By now, people in the city and surrounding community had heard about the moving of God's Spirit. During that revival people came, not just from that community, but across the city and the surrounding areas. Seemingly, most of those coming were not from other churches but curiosity seekers being led by the Spirit. Many received Christ, were later baptized, and eventually raised their families in that church.

These two men became life-long friends. They sang in the choir together, both became Sunday School teachers, and taught new Christians about walking in the Spirit. They were not only willing to forgive each other in unconditional love; they were willing to grow in what we are here calling an authentic relationship.

It is amazing what God can do when we become obedient to God and authentic in our relationship with others.

Questions:

In the story shared above about the history of the church we are wise to recognize that lay leadership and administration are godly gifts for the purpose of ministry. What unique burdens and challenges might people with such gifting carry?

What do you believe caused them to reach out to God in repentance as they did?

What might the leaders in this story have needed to give them courage to become publicly vulnerable and ask for God's help? What did the other members in a congregation need to become publicly vulnerable?

Contemplate:

It is amazing how God can work in our hearts and lives, and in the lives of others, when we let go of our stubborn wills. He is just waiting for us to 'let go'.

Authentic relationships in tomorrow's church will be greatly affected by the authentic relationships in today's church.

Two Worlds - Yet One

It seems like the two key lay influencers in the previous section had different opinions about many things regarding the church, and different preferences about things in life. What they both had in common is what all people have in common. The Holy Spirit is continuously working with us through his Prevenient Grace, Saving Grace, and Sanctifying Grace.

Both Cornelius and Peter experienced Prevenient Grace in their lives. Peter experienced this kind of grace when his brother Andrew introduced him to Jesus (John 1:40-42 NIV). Cornelius experienced this grace as he felt a need to pray to the Jewish God, give offerings, and later when an angel spoke to him. The truth is, we are all so different, but so much the same. The same Holy Spirit draws us. The same Scriptures speak to us. The same Heaven and Hell await all of us depending on whether we decide to follow Christ.

Peter was a Jew. Cornelius was a Gentile. If they were in the same small group, they would at first appear different; however, at a deeper level, they would just have different stories of the Holy Spirit working with them. Two worlds - yet one.

God spoke to Cornelius through an angel and told him to go locate Peter, a Jew, so Peter could come talk to him. It was a disgrace for a Roman soldier to submit to someone else and ask a favor, much less this Jew who was staying overnight in a tanner's house in a place called Joppa. Pentecost had already taken place and, in Peter's thinking, now the Spirit should come to all people. However, after Pentecost, Peter's feelings and prejudice were still lingering and had not entirely changed. In his feeling, he was only comfortable ministering to people who shared his background, opinions, and lifestyle. Meanwhile, the Spirit was drawing the two worlds of Cornelius and Peter together. I think it would have been interesting for the Apostle John to have shown up on the rooftop where Peter was sleeping. He could have reminded Peter, *"For God so loved the world that he gave his one and only Son, that whoever believes in him shall not perish but have eternal life"* (John 3:16 NIV). When Jesus looked down from the cross, there were both centurions and Jews there. Jesus saw one world in which everyone lived, not two or more. All we like sheep have gone astray, and the whole world was broken because of sin.

It was only because of the desire in Cornelius' heart to obey God that he humbled himself to call for Peter. Because of the longing in Peter's heart to obey God, Peter humbled himself to go talk to Cornelius. Those two actions were movements of God to bring the world of the Jews and the Gentiles together.

One of my favorite parts of the story between Cornelius and Peter is when Peter arrived at Cornelius' house and went inside. Cornelius was so spiritually hungry for anything God would bring to him that he knelt in front of Peter and began to worship him. Because of Cornelius' Gentile background, he did not know it was inappropriate to worship a man as though he were a god. Notice what happens next.

When Cornelius, a Roman Centurion, knelt before Peter, Peter, the Jew, did not raise his shoulders back and with pride enjoy the moment. Peter simply told Cornelius, *"…Stand up… 'I am only a man myself'"* (Acts 10:26b NIV). Peter knew of the failures from his own past, his weaknesses as a man of God, and the unthinkable three times he denied his Master. I believe, in that moment when the former world of a Galilean fisherman compared with a career soldier and officer from the army of Rome, Peter understood that we may look like people from two different worlds, but the worlds are only one, in that we both are seeking God. No wonder Peter concluded, *"'I now realize how true it is that God does not show favoritism but accepts men from every nation who fear him and do what is right'"* (Acts 10:34b-35 NIV).

Questions:

Note: when the term "culture" is referred to in the following questions, please apply the questions to cultures outside your country, or cultures within your own country as may be appropriate.

169

Peter and Cornelius were different in many ways. After Cornelius became converted, what might he and Peter have talked about if they went out for coffee or tea?

Peter and Cornelius experienced an authentic relationship with each other. Would they have had to keep in regular contact with each other for the authentic relationship to continue?

When church members meet someone with a different cultural background, do you think most church people come across as proud, or come across as humble, like Peter, when he met Cornelius?

The Holy Spirit communicated to Peter that there were people at the gate, and he needed to go with them. If the Holy Spirit said that to you, what would be your response? How difficult would it be to change your schedule or routine?

Would you be willing to share a story about someone who came into your life or church, who was not a believer, and you felt the Holy Spirit had brought them there, specifically for your spiritual watch care?

Contemplate:

Peter could have remained on the rooftop looking out across the sea, praying, and mentally imagining how much people need Jesus. Instead, through the Spirit, he recognized someone was waiting at the gate.

The church world was changed when Cornelius was converted. Peter was the most influential person in the church world at that time, but he humbled himself, became vulnerable, and put everything on the line to obey the Spirit.

A Scattered Church - Yet One

Peter had the ability to think globally for his day and time. He began his book by writing, *"To God's elect, strangers in the world, scattered throughout Pontus, Galatia, Cappadocia, Asia and Bithynia, who have been chosen according to the foreknowledge of God the Father, through the sanctifying work of the Spirit, for obedience to Jesus Christ and sprinkling by his blood: Grace and peace be yours in abundance"* (I Peter 1:1a-2 NIV).

Those Peter ministered to were mainly Jews, along with a few Gentiles, when Peter describes them all as God's elect. They are strangers because of their overall isolation from other

Christian followers and many have come from locations like Jerusalem to a foreign land. All the places Peter names in the opening verses were in Asia Minor or what would be present day Turkey.

Christians living in those locations truly understood the word persecution. If the persecution was not physical for some, it certainly was emotionally, psychologically, and socially abusive. These men and women of God had turned from their former lives in sin and had begun serving Christ. The costs they paid were enormous in many ways. Socially, they were thought of as evildoers because they did not comply with the surrounding culture. Those in the surrounding culture had developed a deep bitterness and disdain for anyone who questioned if their cultural norms were inappropriate. The followers of Christ were the victims of such bitterness and disgrace. There were many reasons why Christians were considered unacceptable to their culture. One of the complaints was, before the Christians became converted, they would participate in idolatry, sinful celebrations, and immoral living. However, now the opinion of the surrounding culture was that the Christians had abandoned their old friends and the cultural norms that were considered as acceptable behavior for society as a whole. Furthermore, the Christians in Asia Minor were considered as social strangers by those around them because they were living new lives with intentions to model the citizens of Heaven.

Peter, whose name means "rock" or "stone", shares an illustrative picture when he beautifully begins to pull all these followers of Christ from isolated cities and towns together into one large Body of Christ. He refers to them as "living stones" (I Peter 2:5a NIV). Without a doubt, Peter remembered that Jesus had referred to him as a rock or stone. But Peter knew he was not the most important rock, the "Cornerstone" of the church; Jesus was. Instead, Peter saw himself as being just one more of the many stones or strangers, like others brought together into one Body of Christ.

Peter was not entirely alone, and neither were all the countless, isolated strangers in Asia Minor. When Christian friends were absent, to give hope, the Holy Spirit was readily available. When there were few to share authentic relationships with, if any, the Spirit was with them to provide comfort and direction. John was the apostle of love, Paul the apostle of faith, but Peter was the apostle of hope, and he endeavored to encourage others who were suffering for Christ's sake.

For those who did have opportunities to have authentic Christian relationships, Peter had a message for them as well. In I Peter 1:14 NIV, he admonished them to live as obedient children and not return to fulfilling their evil desires when they lived in ignorance. He wanted them to remain authentic in their love for each other and to love one another from the heart (I Peter 1:22 NIV). He knew that feeling isolated and as a stranger could be a dangerous place spiritually. No longer having the support of close friends back in Jerusalem, and now having to live in new relationships, could also cause some to feel sorry for themselves. Relational change is not easy, and Peter warns them in I Peter 2:1 (NIV) to be careful about such things as malice, deceit, hypocrisy, envy, and slander creeping into their relationships. Though isolated, the church needed to remain united and not allow these enemies to fracture the authentic relationships that were continuing.

171

In addition, Peter reminds his followers that Jesus suffered and was rejected by men. Jesus being rejected and having suffered did not mean Jesus was not chosen by God, nor did it mean Jesus was not precious to God. As a matter of fact, Jesus was a living stone infused and strengthened by the same Spirit that brought him from the grave. Now, Peter and all the people of Asia Minor share in the same resurrection power of Jesus. Whether Christians in Jerusalem, Asia Minor, or anywhere else, all Christians are connected by the Holy Spirit.

Those in this world without Christ are dead in their sins, but Christians are alive unto God. Those in this world without Christ are isolated and are the real ones living alone. Those without Christ are not even capable of genuinely relating to others. Those without Christ attempt to merge their selfishness, greed, and power with others while attempting to relate authentically. Christians come together in the Spirit and, because they have died to these things, can receive and give away love, joy, peace, etc., to each other.

A stone building is made up of many stones. Each stone comes from somewhere and has a history all its own. Peter sees the Christians as having stories to tell, and each having experiences seemingly no one else has had. What do living stones have in common? They have a particular purpose, which is to support the Cornerstone. The Cornerstone lines up all the other stones and is the key point of contact so all the other stones can be in a straight line and support the whole building. Peter is saying to all those scattered about, you are not alone. Jesus unites the efforts of every stone throughout Asia Minor and the whole world. Yes, you are isolated, but remember, there are other Christians or stones you have never seen or met.

As a matter of fact, you have never seen or met Jesus personally, but you have an authentic relationship with him. If you trust in Jesus and accept him as the Cornerstone of your relationship, you can trust him that others are connected to him, and all the stones are being arranged for his purpose. The Spirit of Jesus places every stone exactly where it should be and you are part of the House of God. No one is as isolated as you think or feel. By faith, we authentically relate and connect knowing our suffering is not alone, and our labors are not in vain. Authentic relationships consist of more than what you can see or the people you can count. When all alone, or with others, by faith, we can relate to the Chief Cornerstone who is in touch with all other Christians as we are united. I believe Peter sees the House of God as the combined lives, ministries, and efforts of all Christians from all places. This House of God made of living stones is the epicenter of all authentic relationships. All authentic relationships begin with God.

Every person or stone in the House of God is alive by the work of the Holy Spirit. When Christians are all alone and their hands cannot reach far enough to hold one another, by faith, they can be joined to countless other authentic Christian relationships. Peter said, *"As you come to him, the living Stone – rejected by men but chosen by God and precious to him – you also, like living stones, are being built into a spiritual house to be a holy priesthood, offering spiritual sacrifices acceptable to God through Jesus Christ"* (I Peter 2:4-5 NIV).

Questions:

Why do some people feel they will not be able to grow spiritually unless they are continuously relating to and growing along with others?

Should a person attempt to grow spiritually more on their own or with others? If you had to choose, which is the most important to you, and why?

What are the advantages and disadvantages of attempting to grow spiritually on one's own or growing in a group with others? Why?

How do you think Jesus preferred to grow spiritually, being alone or with others? Why?

Is growing spiritually on your own a must before one can be involved in authentic relationships?

Peter described all Christians, wherever they are in the world, as being living stones connected to Jesus, the Chief Cornerstone. Why is it important to continually be aware we are connected and not alone in globally fulfilling the Great Commission?

Contemplate:

People can only be connected to others in godly authentic relationships to the degree they are in a godly authentic relationship with Jesus, the Chief Cornerstone.

It is humbling to realize Jesus chose me to help shape and polish some of the living stones in the house of God.

Being alone with God in an authentic relationship is a rehearsal to prepare us for the next time where two or three are gathered together.

In Closing –

"So this is what the Sovereign Lord says: 'See, I lay a stone in Zion,
a tested stone, a precious cornerstone for a sure foundation;
the one who trusts will never be dismayed.'"
(Isaiah 28:16 NIV)

Jesus is our Chief Cornerstone

Notes:

Made in the USA
Columbia, SC
22 September 2023

23201847R00100